THE WINDS
OF IXTEPEJI

World View and Society

in a Zapotec Town

By

MICHAEL KEARNEY

University of California, Riverside

HOLT, RINEHART AND WINSTON, INC.

NEW YORK   CHICAGO   SAN FRANCISCO   ATLANTA
DALLAS   MONTREAL   TORONTO   LONDON   SYDNEY

Cover: Men, horses, and mules on the road
out of town.

Library of Congress Catalog Card Number: 72–81505
ISBN: 0–03–088457–8
Printed in the United States of America
2 3 4 5 6   059   9 8 7 6 5 4 3 2 1

CASE STUDIES IN
CULTURAL ANTHROPOLOGY

GENERAL EDITORS
George and Louise Spindler
STANFORD UNIVERSITY

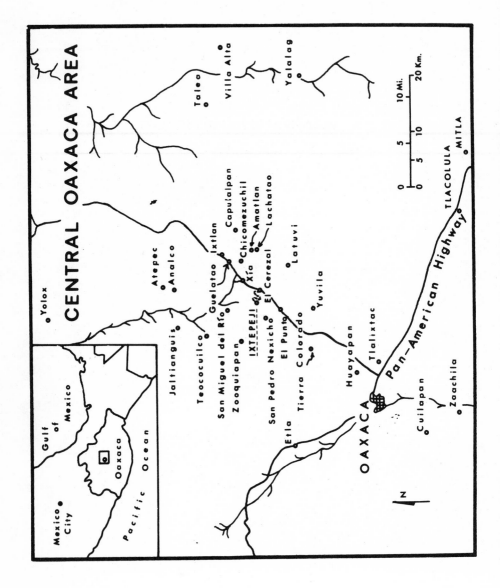

THE WINDS OF IXTEPEJI

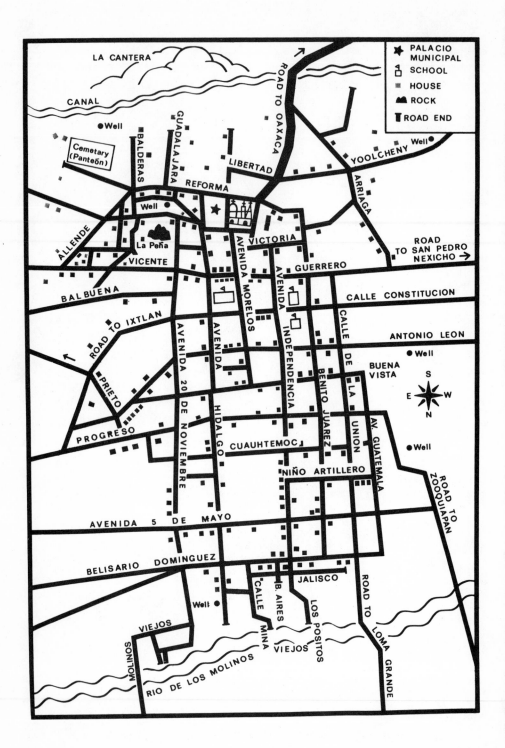

To GEORGE M. FOSTER *and* LAURA NADER

Foreword

About the Series

These case studies in cultural anthropology are designed to bring to students in the social sciences insights into the richness and complexity of human life as it is lived in different ways and in different places. They are written by men and women who have lived in the societies they write about, and who are professionally trained as observers and interpreters of human behavior. The authors are also teachers, and in writing their books they have kept the students who will read them foremost in their minds. It is our belief that when an understanding of ways of life very different from one's own is gained, abstractions and generalizations about social structure, cultural values, subsistence techniques, and other universal categories of human social behavior become meaningful.

About the Author

Michael Kearney received his Ph.D. in anthropology from the University of California, Berkeley, and is now a member of the faculty in the Department of Anthropology at the University of California, Riverside. In 1969–1970 he was a postdoctoral fellow in social psychiatry at the Langley Porter Neuropsychiatric Institute at the University of California Medical Center, San Francisco. In addition to fieldwork in Oaxaca, on which this study is based, he has for several years been studying spiritualistic healing in Baja, California. In his on-going work in Oaxaca he is now conducting a long-range study of peasant farming practices, resource utilization, and mental health. He has published a number of articles based on his work in Mexico and is currently writing a book on Mexican folk medicine and editing a collection of papers in which various anthropologists discuss their fieldwork experiences.

About the Book

This case study deals primarily with the world view and social organization in the Zapotec town of Ixtepeji in the state of Oaxaca, Mexico. The world view is represented by five basic propositions, through which Dr. Kearney expresses underlying motivations prevailing in the system, and in turn relates these to the structural context. In his analysis, the author interrelates folk beliefs and practices with underlying world view. The study is within the realm of cognitive anthropology as the author continually asks, "How do the people perceive their situation?" He depicts their view of reality with interview data and case histories. Although world view is a focus, other salient features of the cultural and social systems are dealt with and interrelated—politics, economics, religion. A complete town history, as well as the townspeople's attitudes about this history, is included.

The title of this study is taken from a dominant set of beliefs related to what is termed the "air system." Ixtepejanos believe that the world, including the air around them, is threatening and filled with dangerous beings, and that one's intimates are also potentially dangerous. One of the basic propositions of the Ixtepejanos' world view places the individual in a real dilemma in interpersonal relationships. It is a basic tenet that humans are susceptible to frustration and envy, which in turn make them wish to harm others. Envy is the main cause of an ailment, called *muina* (evil spirit). One must continually convince others that he is free of *muina* by appearing open and content so that he does not arouse fear and defensive measures in them. For example, if he is really content, he is reluctant to reveal this lest he arouse another person's envy! Thus a great deal of social interaction in Ixtepeji involves the individual managing his impression of himself in order to strike a compromise in this dilemma.

In his social-psychological analysis, Dr. Kearney reveals yet another paradoxical situation, that is, however, quite understandable from the point of view of the Ixtepejanos' own realistic assessment of their conditions of life. Ixtepejanos direct their actions toward adjusting to a world seen as deficient in everything desirable, rather than toward the maximization of desired entities, as might otherwise be expected. Their world view includes the belief that hard work and suffering are inevitable and the Ixtepejanos are too ignorant, weak, and poorly equipped to defend themselves against the harsh environment. They are aware that people in nearby cities and elsewhere live more desirable lives. And, as the author describes, the individual is able to adjust to this otherwise intolerable situation through the use of defensive strategies: repression of desire for the positively valued aspects of life, temporary creation of more ideal environments through drinking, participation in fiestas, disparagement of one's self, and a strong individualistic orientation in interpersonal relations. Thus, as Kearney points out, the social and geographic milieu can be viewed as a complex feedback system in which individuals attempting to protect themselves from threat in the environment take defensive measures which create the very conditions they seek to escape.

Kearney also describes how the current world view, patterns of social interaction, farming practices and technology, and attitudes about the landscape and its resources are obstacles inhibiting economic and social development. He then offers a modest plan to in part offset these problems.

It is impossible for the people of Ixtepeji to attempt prediction of the future or of any changes that might occur since in their view of the world any change is likely to be for the worse. Ixtepejanos are unable to talk about a more desirable future.

The author is aware that the emphases in the study are on the more pathological aspects of life. But, as he writes, "This is how they tell it."

GEORGE AND LOUISE SPINDLER
General Editors

Phlox, Wisconsin

Preface

I first became acquainted with Ixtepeji, the setting of this study, in the summer of 1963, which I spent in the neighboring district of Villa Alta. The fieldwork on which it is based was carried out between December 1965 and June 1967, plus three short visits in July 1969, April 1970, and December 1972.

In order to guard the privacy of those people still living in Ixtepeji whom I have had the audacity to quote or mention, I have changed all names. Therefore, if the name of any living Ixtepejano appears it is only by chance.

Austin, Nevada   MICHAEL KEARNEY
July 1972

Acknowledgments

It would be impossible for me to enumerate here all the people who have helped me bring this work to completion, but I am especially indebted to Laura Nader, who first introduced me to Oaxaca, and to George M. Foster, both of whom offered me continual guidance and inspiration. While working in Oaxaca I have been substantially aided by encouragement and letters of introduction from the late Dr. Eusebio Dávalos Hurtado, Director of the Instituto Nacional de Antropología e Historia and from Dr. Gonzalo Aguirre Beltrán, Director of the Instituto Indígenista Interamericano, both of Mexico City. My thanks also go to Marjorie Fiske Lowenthal, Director of the Adult Development Research Program at the University of California Medical Center in San Francisco, and to Margaret Clark, Senior Anthropologist of the same program that granted me a postdoctoral fellowship from July 1969 to July 1970, thereby providing me the time to return to Ixtepeji in April 1970 and also to prepare this present work for publication. A number of people in Oaxaca also generously provided me with information and assistance of one kind or another, among them Arthur Train, Enrique de la Lanza, Cecil Welte, and Dr. Jorge Fenando Iturribarría. In nearby Ixtlán I have been a guest in the home of Boone Halberg, who has spent many hours with me sharing his intimate knowledge of the area. But without a doubt my greatest debt of gratitude is to the many people of Ixtepeji who so patiently tolerated by intrusion into their lives. It is my sincere hope that the following pages fulfill my promise to them that I would write a book about the town which is at the same time both sympathetic and realistic. Most of all I owe special thanks to the family of Don Valiente Avendaño Guevara and his wife Doña Aurelia Pérez Hernández. Their oldest son Celedonio continues to be my closest friend and coworker in Ixtepeji.

Parts of this work have been published previously elsewhere, in slightly altered form. Chapter 4 appeared in Spanish in *América Indígena*, Vol. 29, pp. 431–450, 1969. The section in Chapter 6 on "The Social Meaning of Food Sharing" has appeared as "The Social Meaning of Food Sharing in Mexico," in *Kroeber Anthropological Society Papers*, Fall 1970, pp. 32–41. Chapter 9 appeared as "Drunkenness and Religious Conversion in a Mexican Village," in the *Quarterly Journal of Studies on Alcohol*, Vol. 31, pp. 132–152, 1970. Chapter 10 appeared as "La Llorona as a Social Symbol," in *Western Folklore*, Vol. 28, pp. 199–206, 1969. And parts of the section in Chapter 11 on "Emotions and Philosophy of Life" are from "An Exception to the 'Image of Limited Good,'" *American Anthropologist*, Vol. 71, pp. 888–890, 1969.

Contents

THE WINDS OF IXTEPEJI

1

Introduction

HIS STUDY deals with world view and social organization in the Zapotec town of Ixtepeji (eeks-tay-páy-he), in the state of Oaxaca (wa-há-ca), Mexico. It examines certain folk beliefs of the people of Ixtepeji and how these ideas relate to social structure, politics, religion, and so on. The main topic is how the people perceive reality and how such perceptions affect, and in turn are affected by, the conduct of village life, which is described in local and historical context.

The title is taken from one dominant set of beliefs that have to do with what can be called the "air system." This is a complex of ideas, sentiments, and practices that circumscribe large segments of world view and values.

The organization of this book is as follows: Chapter 2 sketches the socio-cultural and geographic setting of the town, while Chapter 3 outlines the town history and the townspeople's attitudes about this history. Chapter 4 presents the salient aspects of world view in the form of five basic propositions, each of which is the basis for the subsequent five chapters, which continue through Chapter 9. Whereas each of these five chapters deals with specific aspects of Ixtepeji world view and society, Chapters 10 and 11 demonstrate how they all are functionally interdependent by using them to analyze several folks beliefs and practices. Thus Chapter 10 deals with the extensive use of alcohol in Ixtepeji, while Chapter 11 interprets a common folk tale. In these two chapters, as throughout the entire study, there is an emphasis on the relationship between folk beliefs and practices and the underlying world view propositions. As the reader will soon discover, life is difficult in Ixtepeji, and is so perceived by the people themselves; Chapter 12 discusses how they adjust to such a sociopsychological and physical environment. Finally, Chapter 13 discusses some implications of present world view and social patterns for culture change in Ixtepeji.

1

The Town of Ixtepeji

Cultural and Geographic Setting

NORTH EAST of Oaxaca City, the Sierra Juárez rises abruptly almost without foothills from the Valley of Oaxaca. The main access into the Sierra is a road, which was opened in the mid-1930s, that leaves the Pan American Highway five kilometers south of Oaxaca City. After an initial steep climb from the semiarid valley, it continues to wind upward through moister and often fog-enshrouded pine forests, soon crossing the Continental Divide and dropping down through the *monte* of Ixtepeji. After crossing several deep canyons, descent into each of which is accompanied by extreme ecological changes, it arrives at the small town of Guelatao, birthplace of Benito Juárez, whose name the region bears. Here the pavement ends, but the road continues for 162 kilometers through the nearby town of Ixtlán, the seat of the district of the same name, and over another series of mountains until it reaches Tuxtepec, near the border of Vera Cruz.

Ixtepeji lies on a northern mountain slope 4.5 kilometers north of the road, 37 kilometers after it leaves the Pan American Highway, or a little over half the distance to Ixtlán. The usual entry into the town is by a steep dirt road, passable only for heavy-duty trucks and four-wheel-drive vehicles. The *municipio* of Ixtepeji, of which the town is the center, is one of twenty-eight municipios forming the district of Ixtlán. It is bounded on the north by the municipios of San Miguel del Río and Jaltianquis, and on the south by those of Huayapan and Tlalixtac de Cabrera; the eastern boundaries are San Juan Chicomezúchil and Lachatao, and the western ones are Teococuilco, Santiago Zooquiapan, and San Pablo Etla. The entire municipio has a population of about 2200, of whom 1200 to 1300 live in Ixtepeji; these figures vary, however, because many people divide their time between the town and a second residence, or *rancho*, in the mountains around the town. In addition to the center, four other settlements in the municipio are categorized as *agencias* (Tierra Colorado, El Punto, Yuvila, and San Pedro Nexicho), and eleven as *rancherias* (El Cebollal, La Ex-Hacienda de San Jerónimo, La Cienega, La Cumbre, La Palma, Manzanillo, El Cerezal, Yoo-Vaneli, Xielavé, Reynoso, and Xía). Also, according to older people who are interested in such things, the name Ixtepeji derives from the Aztec *Ixtliptepji* (the precipice where there is obsidian).

The Zapotec term for the original settlement, which was located on a flat at the lower end of the present town, is *Latzi-yela* (field by the lagoon), a term that is also occasionally applied to the present settlement.

Besides the main road that goes up to the highway, Ixtepeji is connected with neighboring settlements by a number of trails that radiate out from it. The antiquity of some of these is verified by the depths to which they have eroded into the ground, often completely swallowing a mounted man. Prehistorically, from the Colonial Period, and to the present, these were the routes traveled by the Zapotec traders who are the traditional itinerant merchants of the region.

Besides frequent journeys made to Oaxaca City and neighboring towns by the mobile Ixtepejanos, twice-weekly mail deliveries, which are collected by a runner to Ixtlán, maintain communication with the outside. Also, in November 1965, a telephone line was strung between the municipio and the district seat in Ixtlán. There had been a telegraph line to Oaxaca City, but it was destroyed in 1911, at the beginning of the Revolution, and never replaced.

In the sixteenth century, the Spaniards congregated neighboring Indian groups in Ixtepeji to extract tribute and later to supply labor for gold and silver mines near the town. Ixtepejanos are quick to explain how hard times, which have continued until the present, came upon them during that period. The conditions of the generations of servitude to the Spanish overlords changed little after the Mexican independence (in the early 1800s), by which time the town came under the domination of a series of local *caciques*, or strong men, who ruled the Ixtepejanos with severity equal to the Spaniards. This long history of domination reached a catastrophic climax in 1912, in the early days of the Mexican Revolution, when, due to the vicissitudes of local politics, a military detachment, amply assisted by volunteers from neighboring towns, attacked the town with cannons and small arms. After a bloody resistance many of the surviving men of the town were impressed into the army and sent off to fight in the northern campaigns of the Revolution. With no opposition to resist them, the townspeople from the neighboring communities descended upon Ixtepeji to plunder it, tumbling over the walls of the houses, searching for hidden savings, and driving the remaining population into exile.

The town was not resettled until 1921, after ten years of almost constant war, when the area was quiet enough so that the survivors could return. Although the events of the Revolution freed the Ixtepejanos, they left a generalized social and economic disruption from which the town has not yet recovered. The people of Ixtepeji point to the old mines, as well as to the rather impressive pre-Columbian ruins and other relics of the past, as evidence of how much better conditions were formerly and how hard times are now. Old ruined grain mills and a foundry along the road to Oaxaca, as well as overgrown threshing floors still found in the fields and woods, are further testaments to the more abundant harvests and wealth of times past. The people also point out that the lands around town are being progressively deforested so that each year firewood becomes more scarce, and the land more dry and eroded. But one of the bitterest blows of recent history is the increased growth and prosperity of Ixtepeji's historic rival, Ixtlán. Whereas Ixtepeji had been the cultural and economic center of the Sierra Juárez, it is now of conspicuously lesser significance than Ixtlán and several other nearby towns. In addition to the military conquest of Ixtepeji, its cultural and economic reversal was furthered when, in the 1930s, a road into the Sierra was opened, which by-passed the town. The road, however, does go to Ixtlán and is largely responsible for its recent prosperity and growth.

In discussing recent historic events, Ixtepejanos emphasize the terrors of war, their desire for peace and security, and their fears of both internal and external conflicts. This desire for harmony and peace comes out as a strongly expressed value for internal unity and solidarity at whatever cost.

Aside from their historic misfortunes, Ixtepejanos also perceive their present lives' conditions in a negative light. In general, there is a feeling that they are being left behind by the rest of the world, where conspicuous positive changes are observable. They perceive the local environment as essentially lacking in natural resources sufficient for anything above mere subsistence. Individuals, especially unmarried young people, face the dilemma of remaining in the municipio, or leaving its minimal security to seek their fortunes in the outside world—the realm of a possibly better life, but also an unknown, fearful place where the unsophisticated villager realistically sees that he is at a great disadvantage. Those who remain, and they are the greater majority, must deal with the problem of adjusting to the perceived harsh realities of the local setting. In describing it, Ixtepejanos stress several qualities. First there is the poverty, which is believed to be increasing, due to the diminishing supply of natural resources (caused by soil erosion and deforestation), which in turn reduces the town's watershed, which is necessary for irrigation in the dry winter months. In addition to these physical and economic conditions, townspeople also dwell on the emotional quality of the environment, which is pervaded with *tristeza* (sadness) and *soledad* (solitude). The affective connotations of these terms are hard to translate. Essentially they refer to a melancholy, immobilized, shadowy, quiet milieu, which envelops the lonely individual who forever desires to escape to a setting filled with *alegría* (happiness) and *movimiento* (movement, action). The city, with its bustle of business, noise, and bright lights, is seen, aside from its potential dangers, as the epitome of these qualities.

Ixtepeji, today, is a town of peasant farmers. Virtually the entire population devotes itself to the cultivation of corn, beans, and other staples of the rural Mesoamerican diet. All production is at or near a subsistence level, due to the mountainous topography, inefficient techniques, and scarcity of irrigation water. What individual cash income there is comes mainly from secondary activities such as hauling and trading coffee and other crops grown in nearby areas, manufacturing and selling charcoal, operating small stores, carpentry, masonry, folk curing, and witchcraft. Recently there has been limited intermittent work cutting timber for a paper company that has been logging in the mountains above the town.

The town's limited water supply flows to it, from a source in the mountains, in a narrow canal originally constructed in pre-Columbian times; it is no more than a foot wide, several inches deep, and 5800 meters long. Except for small seeping springs, this canal supplies all the water for the entire town. In 1966–1967 a pipe system, fed by the canal, was laid with fifteen faucets. Shortly after completion, however, slippage of the earth began to break the pipes, so that the system was still not in operation in 1970, nor was it foreseeable that funds for repairs would be available.

The town is a "face to face" community; except for small children everyone knows everyone else by sight and name, and is able to trace extensive family networks. This stems in part from a high incidence of town endogamy, a tendency influenced by Ixtepeji having long been in armed opposition to neighboring towns, and in part from the relatively small size of the community.

Of the three general systems of land tenure in Mexico—a pre-Columbian communal system, individual private ownership introduced by the Spanish, and the *ejido* system of post-Revolutionary land reforms—only the first is formally recognized in Ixtepeji. As in pre-Columbian times title to all land is legally vested in the community and is administered by the elected officials. There is, however, individual tenure by right of use. Any *comunero* (adult member of the community) is free to utilize any unoccupied land. It is treated as his alone for as long as he cares to exploit it. Therefore, land can neither be sold nor inherited, except for house plots, which, as with houses, are treated in practice as private property held in *fee simple*. All comuneros also have the right to hunt on municipal land and cut wood for firewood and charcoal. The right to use land in the municipio is attainable virtually only by birth or marriage into the community. In the past there have been a number of bitter land disputes between towns of the Sierra, and Ixtepejanos today zealously maintain their municipal boundary by regularly repairing land markers and clearing the boundary line of all plant growth—a formidable task considering the length and width of the swath.

The first formal schooling began after resettlement of the town in 1921, when one teacher was in residence. Some years later another was added, and one more in 1935. Since 1944 there have been either six or seven teachers in the town teaching the full primary curriculum of six years.

Today the population is in varying degrees bilingual in Spanish and a dialect of *serrano* Zapotec. Spanish is spoken predominantly, especially by the younger adults and their children, and by adults participating in most affairs transacted in the town hall.

Except for Ixtlán, there is less Zapotec spoken in Ixtepeji than in other Sierra towns. Ixtepejanos themselves explain this by saying that when the population was dispersed in 1912, most of them got used to speaking only Spanish and continued to do so when they returned. They also explain that many people born out of town at this time learned little Zapotec as children. Despite this relative loss of the local language, however, many men of the town who have trading relations farther back in the mountains speak other Zapotec dialects.

Ixtepeji's local reputation has three characteristics: 1) Continuing in their Zapotec heritage, many men of the town are *arrieros*, or muleteers, who trade throughout the area, their main routes running from Oaxaca City into the mountains to the east. The extent of this part-time occupation derives from Ixtepeji's

Sowing corn. (Note the armadillo shell used to hold seeds.)

geographic position at the hub of ancient trails and from the fact that it is the first main town in the Sierra Juárez, often referred to as "the door to the Sierra." 2) More important than their reputation as muleteers is their infamous identity as the "rebels of the Sierra." This epithet comes from events in the Revolutionary period that culminated in the destruction of the town and the dispersal of the population. 3) The third characteristic of Ixtepejanos is that they are good musicians, a specialty that results in large part from the songs they learned during the years they wandered in exile.

Man and the Land

Whether one is looking at a panorama of Ixtepeji from a far mountain, or studying a collection of utensils or tools, land use patterns, the daily round of life, the annual economic cycle, the nutrition of the people, or their dreams, there is one thing that is always present, and that is corn. It is ironic that this crop, the pedestal upon which human life in the town so precariously perches, should be so ill adapted to the precipitous slopes and fragile soils of the region. Whereas corn provided a fruitful adaptation to this same area in the pre-Columbian past, current human practices and requirements have disrupted the ancient agricultural systems

Shucking corn.

that existed before Hernán Cortés became the Marquis of the Valley of Oaxaca. Corn cultivation as it developed in tropical Mexico is best practiced extensively with a dispersed population that does not exert strong pressure on the regenerative power of the land. In the Sierra Juárez a trend away from this began when the Spaniards congregated the Indians into denser settlements. And then, as it is now, the land was further violated with Spanish plows which gouge long furrows in fields cleared with metal axes. And today fallow fields are further tortured by the sharp hooves of European cattle, horses, mules, and burros, which retard new growth of grasses, brush, and trees. The most obivous and pernicious effect of these practices is severe soil erosion. As a response to this the people use the rocks exposed by the torrential rains to partially terrace some fields. But gaping "V" shaped gullies and muddy rivulets and rivers swollen by summer rains belie their effectiveness.

The narrow margin of security that the corn-based economy provides was recently demonstrated. In July and August of 1969 unusually heavy rains, lasting for over forty days virtually without stop, severely damaged the corn crop and caused considerable erosion. The following autumn many families had no harvest and were thus forced to buy corn in Oaxaca City at inflated prices. To do so many men of the municipio were either forced into debt or forced to leave the area to look for temporary employment.[1]

Corn cultivation, as Ixtepejanos presently practice it, is, through erosion and soil exhaustion, constantly diminishing the base on which they depend for their livelihoods. To Ixtepejanos the most poignant and threatening effect of this trend is that there is no longer a sufficient amount of good arable land to support all those born into the municipio, which, between 1960 and 1970, decreased in population from 2251 to 2216. The town of Ixtepeji itself decreased from 1328 to 1237, while some of the other settlements increased only slightly. During the same period there were 1131 live births and 504 deaths recorded in the entire municipio. Adding the difference between births and deaths to the 1960 population and then subtracting the 1970 population reveals 662 persons not accounted for in the 1970 census and who have therefore presumably left the municipio during the previous ten years. This figure averages out to an emigration rate of 3 percent per year.[2]

It is bad enough that history and poverty have imposed inadequate agricultural practices on the people, but conditions are worsened by the absence of other agricultural techniques that could in part offset such misuse of the land. The use of fertilizers is virtually nonexistent, except that some attempt is made to tether animals in fields after harvesting so that they may eat some of the fodder and leave

---

[1] This same year the neighboring town of Zooquiapan was so severely damaged by heavy rains that the residents decided to relocate the entire town to the top of a nearby ridge out of fear that another such deluge would wash it off the mountainside.

[2] The average birth rate in the municipio between 1960 and 1970 was 50.6 per thousand as compared with a national rate of about 46 per thousand. The average death rate for the same period was 22.6 per thousand, which is considerably higher than the national rate of about 12 per thousand. The rate of population growth between 1960 and 1970 (not excluding emigrants) averages out to 2.8 percent per year, which being only slightly lower than the emigration rate of 3.0 percent results in a nearly stable population. The total area of the municipio is 21,059 hectares and has a population density of 27.3 persons per square mile.

Erosion and land slippage in a milpa.

their manure, a large part of which is washed off with the first rains. In terms of getting organic material into the soil it would be better to plow under the fodder, but the simple wooden plow is not designed to do this, as are steel moldboard plows, which are not in use in Ixtepeji and which would presumably cause even greater erosion if they were. In any event, the fodder is a major food for work animals and as such it is not available to be plowed back into the soil. Also, crop rotation is absent as a perceived beneficial technique. Instead, fields are cultivated until they no longer produce an acceptable harvest and are then left fallow for a year or two in the case of *solares* in the town or, if they are in monte, until they have been overgrown by natural vegetation. Although Ixtepejanos, both men and women, have encyclopedic knowledge of local flora and its uses, it is alarming that they are unaware of such basic agricultural practices. Once while helping some friends shell corn I came across a particularly well formed ear and asked them if they would like to put it aside for seed. "No," they replied, "that's a good one to eat; any kernel will do for planting." Later I discovered that this was a common attitude and practice.

In order to prepare the soil and plant it, especially in the short time available in unirrigated fields, plowing must be done with oxen (rather than doing it by hand, which causes less erosion). Because of his dependence on corn the Ixtepejano is bound to his oxen almost as surely as he yokes them to his crude home-made plow. And even if it were economically possible to cultivate with tractors, the inclination of the slopes would make them useless in many fields. When one thinks of other societies such as Nilotic peoples of North Africa, or rice farmers of Asia who also live in symbiotic relationships with other varieties of these placid, powerful beasts, and have in some cases built their economies around them, the Ixtepejanos's relatively insignificant utilization of them is puzzling. Although well trained to plow they are not used as beasts of burden, nor are they milked (no one drinks milk in Ixtepeji except for small amounts of powdered milk occasionally given to children), nor does anyone today use their hides. And since they usually die unnoticed while turned loose to graze in the monte, they are virtually never eaten, except when an occasional one is slaughtered for a fiesta.

It is in the face of such handicaps that the people plant and harvest their uncooperative lands, which they classify according to climate and altitude. The most productive lands are the comparatively few solares and *milpas* of the *tierra templada* (temperate zone) in and around the town itself. They are desirable for their relative levelness and nearness, and the availability of water for irrigation,

Yoked oxen carrying plow.

which allows for *cultivo de riego* as opposed to the greater extent of arable land which is *de temporal*, that is, dependent on the vagaries of the rainfall. The town lies at an elevation of about 6500 to 7000 feet, while the mountains above it rise up to over 8000 feet, where lower temperatures and more rainfall support mixed pine and oak forests. Here in *tierra fría* (cold zone) a more traditional slash-and-burn farming is practiced, with planting and harvesting usually done a month or so later than at the lower elevation. The third and least productive zone is the *tierra caliente* (hot zone), which is down in the canyons of several rivers.

Settlement Pattern and Housing

Throughout the early Colonial period in Spanish America old settlements were reorganized and new towns created with great uniformity according to principles first drawn up by Greek and then later by Roman city planners. The layout of Ixtepeji looks as though some seventeenth century Spanish officer attempted to impose this plan on the steep contours of the original pre-Columbian settlement. Looking down onto the town one sees a rough grid work of unpaved streets, five of them running vertically up and down the mountain in a north–south direction and crossed perpendicularly by ten others. But toward the periphery this regularity gives way to a more convenient meandering of streets and paths. As was standard,

Church and two-story municipal building behind it, located above the center of town.

House in fallow milpas.

the town was originally divided into four quarters, or *barrios*, by two streets that intersect in the center of the town, with a supernumary barrio later appended to the west edge. Although barrio membership is now scrambled geographically, the original boundaries are still recognized. A *zócalo*, or public square, which is so prominent throughout the nation, is conspicuously absent in the town. An imposing Colonial church, which according to Royal directives should have been placed in the center of the town, is above it on a site that could be leveled with reasonable effort.

In Ixtepeji, as elsewhere, settlement pattern and architecture are to some extent an expression of personality and values. Ixtepejanos prefer privacy, but not isolation, in their private lives. Accordingly, the community is neither densely compact nor a so-called vacant town such as is found among the neighboring Mixe Indians and in other areas of southern Mexico. Each home is typically on a solar of about one half of an hectare, which may be planted with the ubiquitous corn and beans and most likely some alfalfa, a few fruit trees and possibly some gladiolas or other crops that need irrigation and special care. Most of the houses consist of one room and, except for the very poorest, are constructed of large sun-dried adobe bricks and mud mortar. They are substantial structures that endure for generations if the walls are protected from the rains, which otherwise wash them back into the earth in several years. The front wall is usually raised higher than the rear. Log rafters are laid on the tops of the walls, sloping from front to back. Across these are laid horizontal thin boards to support curved tiles or, more common in recent years, sheets of corrugated tar paper or aluminum. A lower second set of horizontal rafters is usually built into the walls, spanning the interior. Across these are lashed cane stalks which form a flooring substantial enough to support the ton or so of corn that the family will consume from one harvest to the next. On the outside and in front, a sloping roof with open sides provides additional work and storage area. These houses may have from one to three windows with wooden shutters but no glass panes. The dim interior is apt to be further obscured by irritating smoke from a hearth that is on the floor in one corner, or perhaps raised up on a platform of adobe bricks. Against the opposite wall is the most imposing item in the house, the family altar, decorated with a canopy of crepe paper, flowers, colored tinsel, ribbons, and moss. Here one prays and makes offerings to the saints and the spirits of dead relatives, and when one dies he is stretched out on it for his wake.

Several families have beds; everyone else sleeps on *petates* laid out on planks elevated from the ground or rolled out on the dirt floor. Almost everyone sleeps in his clothes, rolled up in a blanket, brothers with brothers, sisters with sisters, and small children with the parents.

The most common improvement made on houses is the construction of a separate kitchen, most likely of *tejamanil* (long narrow shingles), cane, and perhaps some unmortared bricks. Building expenses are usually further minimized by having it share a common wall with the house. About one half of the families in Ixtepeji have this type of separate kitchen. After a separate kitchen the next most likely improvement is electrification, which usually means bare 40- or 50-watt light bulbs dangling in the kitchen and main room, and a radio. In recent years, in some of the wealthier homes there is also apt to be an electric iron or food blender.

Health and Illness

Although house construction is ecologically sound in that the main construction material, earth, is plentiful and inexpensive, house design and use is

Houses and fields in the lower part of town.

not conducive to good health. The high roofs and thick walls that keep them cool in the hot spring and summer months are cold, damp, and drafty in the winter when people have the flu and respiratory ailments. Cracks in the walls and open windows provide free access to rats and mice, which are attracted to the corn stores and food left overnight around the hearth. Often on their nocturnal scurrying these rodents run across the faces of those asleep in the house. Also, with a virtual complete absence of privies the people avail themselves of the areas immediately surrounding the house. This practice in turn maintains endemic dysentery and intestinal parasite infestation which, according to visiting doctors and municipal death certificates, is the greatest cause of death. The main avenues of infection are flies and water contamination. Intestinal ailments are usually highest in the wet season when maggots are hatching and the rain overflowing from the fields and streets runs into the ditches and water holes. Once taken from these unsanitary sources household water is stored in large open *ollas* where it is further contaminated by utensils left on the floor. Although copious quantities of sweetened coffee are drunk with each meal it is barely brought to a boil and there is a common belief that boiled water is appropriate only for a person who is already sick. Infants and small children are especially prone to stomach problems since they spend much time crawling and toddling on the moist earth kitchen floors among constantly intruding chickens, turkeys, and dogs, and as with babies everywhere, everything goes into their mouths. After weaning mothers usually feed their children on the floor also, placing their bowls directly on the ground.

Girls getting household water.

In 1965–1966 the town had the service of its first resident doctor, a recent medical graduate, a *pasante*, who performed seven months of civil service medical care for the people of the municipio. This was fortunate timing as there was a local epidemic of smallpox and a severe regional influenza epidemic during this period. The people were quick to point out, however, that these were nothing compared to a typhoid fever epidemic in 1944, which is reported to have killed 200 people in the municipio. Earlier, in 1940, there was an epidemic of measles that reputedly killed over 100 persons, and more recently between 1964 and 1967, there were again numerous deaths attributed to the same disease. Since 1968 those part-time workers employed by the previously mentioned paper company have had available to them the intermittent services of doctors from the Mexican Institute of Social Security.

Diet

The diet is in general typical of most of rural southern Mexico. The fare of the typical household in Ixtepeji appears to contain all that is necessary for sound nutrition, but varying degrees of malnutrition result from a disproportionately high intake of corn tortillas and beans, often the only solid food eaten for days at a time. Corn provides the greater part of caloric intake (*cf.* Chapter 7) while a variety of beans are the main source of protein. Plant protein is supplemented by occasional eggs, turkey, chicken, pig, and less often by ox and horse meat, fish, and wild game. Local streams yield no fish, but dried fish and canned sardines are occasionally purchased in Oaxaca and apparently account for the absence of goiters, which are noticeable in other areas of the Sierra Juárez. Wild animals—doves, song birds, possum, and deer—are also a significant source of animal protein, especially for poorer families. As mentioned earlier, fresh milk is not drunk, although mothers sometimes give powdered milk to children. Nor does anyone in the municipio prepare cheese, although Ixtepejanos occasionally buy it elsewhere.

A number of tree crops are grown locally, although most of them in small quantities—peach, apple, pear, quince, plum, orange, lime, sweet lemon, walnut, pomegranate, and cherry. Other tree products are also available through nearby markets and find their way into Ixtepeji kitchens—papaya, avocado, banana, *zapote, chicozapote, guajilote, cherimoya* (soursop), *mamey,* cacao, and coffee.

Other food plants, most of which are not grown locally, are a variety of squashes, chiles, onions, pineapples, tomatoes, potatoes, garlic, and blackberries. The semidomesticated *chayote* grows locally as do several cacti, the latter of which is more apt to be served when little else is available. A great variety of leafy plants and seeds are either grown or purchased, such as mint, coriander, parsley, or gathered wild and eaten with meals or used medicinally. Whenever in the fields or forests, both men and women are alert to whatever edible wild plants can be cut and carried home. The availability of wild edibles is one likely reason that truck gardening has not developed in Ixtepeji.

There is much irregularity in the presence of all these foods other than corn and beans in all households throughout the year due to seasonal crop variation and the changing economic condition of families. Irregularity of household supply is noticeably greater in Ixtepeji than in other comparable towns that have markets which provide a more constant selection of nonlocal foods. In contrast, Ixtepeji households may often go for long periods on a monotonous diet of essentially corn and beans suddenly to be glutted with avocados, tomatoes, or some other crop brought home in bulk by men of the house who have gone to haul cargo in some other region.

Noticeable dietary changes are now occurring, most of them apparently bad. Locally cooked, nonenriched white bread, usually eaten stale is said to be more common than in former years. And whereas chocolate, fruit drinks, and coffee were formerly sweetened with raw sugar, many families are now using white sugar which is of course without nutritional benefit and most likely a significant cause of the present high rate of dental caries in children. Also on the increase is the consumption of bottled soft drinks and beer, which are reducing the intake of the native fermented drink *tepache*, which is undoubtedly more nutritious. The use of the distilled liquor *mezcal* appears, however, to be unaffected by the new beverages (re tepache and mezcal *cf.* Chapter 10).

Formal Organization

If the social life of the town be thought of as an organism, it is its formal groups which are its bones, the structure upon which hangs the flesh of daily life, religion, and fiestas. It is also in this formal organization that some of the strongest symbols of town identity and unity are found. Whereas there is little informal social organization in the sense of voluntary associations or mutual aid arrangements, there is much active participation in the municipal government and church administration.

As in much of rural Mexico, local government and church administration in Ixtepeji is executed by elected, nonpaid officials. In Ixtepeji there is no distinction in actual practice between participation in church and government roles. Together they constitute a more or less fixed hierarchy of offices called *cargos* in which all able bodied men must participate as a requisite for living in the municipio. Young men enter the hierarchy by fulfilling some of the less significant cargos and progress to those of more responsibility. A man's major cargo serving career begins at age eighteen if he is married or at twenty-one if he is single, and lasts until he is sixty, at which time he is automatically known as a *principal*—a man who has fulfilled his obligations to the municipio and no longer must serve cargos, contribute to collections, or attend town meetings.

Municipal cargos are filled by appointment of the minor ones by each of the five barrios, or wards (see below), of the town, and election of the major ones at a general meeting. Cargos are generally recognized as an unavoidable consequence of living in the municipio. However, there are ways to avoid them. A fairly common tactics for avoiding a cargo is for a likely candidate to leave town for a few months around the time of the elections, or as one person put it, "only until this blow that we receive here has passed." On occasions individuals pay up to 2000 pesos to get a substitute for a minor cargo, but such a practice is strongly disapproved of and is not acceptable in the case of the more important ones. Although it is true that the amount of personal work one may do while he is on active duty with a cargo is limited, many men are apt to overstress this point. Absence from duty of any cargo is fined, unless an excuse is accepted. At times absentees who have previously submitted written requests to be excused are checked to verify that they have in fact been incapable of appearing. The higher cargos do seriously limit the amount of gainful work that a man can engage in, but none of them completely prevents him from engaging in his usual activities. Since the amount of attention he can give to his personal work is greatly reduced, the burden of a cargo, if not anticipated and prepared for, or if untoward events suddenly arise in his personal life, may place a man in heavy debt by the end of his term. In general, a man is allowed two years of rest after serving a minor cargo and three years after serving a major one.

The most honored cargo is that of *presidente*. The man in this office serves as the formal head of the municipio. He is the one who represents it in most dealings with the outside and who presides over local civic events.

Second in prestige and authority to the presidente is the *síndico*. He is, loosely speaking, the attorney general of the municipio, and in this capacity is the

Officials of municipal government.

local representative of his counterpart at the district level, the *agente del ministerio público*, to whom he is directing responsible for investigating criminal actions, and imposing punishment or adjusting claims in the case of minor crimes and disputes. Both he and the presidente have the power to impose fines and place people in the dungeon-like jail cells (one for men and one for women) of the *ayuntamiento* (town hall) for several days or, in the case of men, to punish them with up to three days of public work. In addition to working with the presidente to settle disputes brought to the ayuntamiento, the síndico must organize and direct the frequent *tequios*, which are work parties composed of men of the municipio. But his main responsibility is to protect the integrity of the community legally, not only in inter-community disputes, but also in any complications that involve the town as a whole. As such, he must make frequent trips to Ixtlán and Oaxaca City to deal with usually more sophisticated people and then come back and be responsible for his perform-ance to the townspeople. Regarding disputes that he must mediate within the town, Ixtepejanos point out that in many cases it is impossible for him not to make enemies when a decision must be made either one way or the other. The síndico usually gets the brunt of such cases since the presidente tends to pass them on to him, as is his prerogative according to town custom.

Both the presidente and síndico are elected for three years, but in practice serve for only eighteen months, their substitutes, or *suplentes*, taking over for the following eighteen months.

Often working closely with the presidente and síndico are the *regidores*, of which there are ten, plus ten suplentes. They serve mainly in an advisory capa-city to the other officers, and often decisions are made in the name of the presidente or síndico after they have discussed them with the regidores. Two of the regidores, referred to as *primer* and *secundo regidor*, are the most active, and the primer regidor has the obligation of sponsoring a fiesta in Holy Week for all men asso-ciated with the ayuntamiento and church hierarchy for that year. The term of the regidores is also for three years, but, as with the presidente and síndico, it is split between the regidores and their suplentes.

Another major cargo is that of the *comisario de bienes comunales*, who is responsible for the communal property of the municipio. It is he who grants requests for use rights to communal lands and who adjudicates disputes over land. He is also responsible for protecting the interests of the municipio in its dealings with a paper company that is cutting wood in the municipio. He is assisted by a treasurer, a secretary, and a council of representatives made up of men of the agen-cias. As with the other higher cargos, these last for three years, and are likewise in practice split between two men. They are of particular interest, however, since a small salary, paid by the paper company, goes along with them.

The office of *alcalde*, or mayor, seems to have decreased in importance in recent years and now serves mainly minor ceremonial functions. This is a one-year cargo, which is split between the alcalde and his suplente into two six-month terms. To handle the sheaves of bureaucratic paper work that often smother municipal officers, there are three secretaries (always male)—two *secretarios municipales* and one *secretario de alcalde*, all three of whom serve together for one year.

One of the most onerous cargos is that of *tesorero*, or treasurer, since the man fulfilling it is in the delicate position of having to handle and account for municipal funds. Bearing the responsibility for this money, he constantly runs the liability of a shortage and the accusation of having used it for himself, "of having eaten it," as it is common to say. His moment of truth comes at the end of his one-year term when, at a general assembly, he presents the balance to the town and reads off a list of all collections and expenses. At this time, the townspeople listen to see that their fines and assessments have been properly recorded and to complain if they have not.

The policing of the town is the direct duty of the *comandante del pueblo*. He has under his direction twenty young men referred to as *topiles*, and five others of higher rank called *comandantes de policía*, or *mayores de vara*. This group is collectively known as the policía, and its main duties consist of calming violent disputes, apprehending people accused of crimes or misdeeds, and subduing drunken men. This group is coordinated in a system of rotation whereby four topiles and one comandante are on duty twenty-four hours a day. When not engaged in some actual duty, they are usually lounging around the town hall where they are at the beck and call of the higher officials whose commands are relayed through the comandante on duty.

In the absence of a resident priest, a group of cargo holders known as the *Junta Vecinal* is responsible for the maintenance of the church. These men are headed by a president, also referred to as the *sacristán mayor*, who, along with his vice-president and two honorary officers called *fiscales*, directs the activities of and works with eight sacristans who, as the topiles and comandantes de policía, are appointed by the barrios. Collectively they are responsible for the church and several plots of land cultivated for church expenses. At least two sacristans are on duty at all times; at night they sleep in the ruins of an old rectory where they are available to toll the church bells and let people in to pray. Another traditional obligation of the sacristán mayor is to provide the tepache for the Holy Week fiesta. Whereas the Junta Vecinal is mainly responsible for the upkeep of the church and its day-to-day functioning, special religious events are mainly funded and carried out either by individual sponsors, the barrios (see below), or the town as a whole.

There are several other minor municipal cargos that last for one year. Two men referred to as *alguaciles* regularly patrol the long canal that brings water to town from the mountains, looking for leaks and clearing it of debris. Two others, also appointed for one year, are known as *guardamontes*. They make irregular tours around the limits of the municipio to check boundary markers and to look for violations of land use.

In the outlying agencias of the municipio, municipal authority is represented by *agentes municipales* who are elected by the inhabitants of each agencia, and who are assisted by two local topiles.

In the municipio there are also chosen representatives of the ruling national political party, the Institutional Revolution Party (PRI), and two of its supporting organizations, the National Peasants' Confederation (CNC) and the National Confederation of Popular Organizations (CNOP). Each administration of the municipio regularly declares itself in support of PRI. No opposition activity whatsoever is ever manifested in the municipio, mainly out of fear of being identified as a rebel town and thus incurring the disfavor of PRI officials in Oaxaca City who control government patronage in the state.

In addition to the above municipal and religious cargos there is an Education Committee (*Comité Educativo*), which in practice functions as two distinct groups—an all male League of Parents (*Liga de Padres de Familia*) and the Feminine League of Education (*Liga Feminil de Educación*). These groups maintain the school and prepare occasional fiestas for the children and teachers. Their operating expenses are earned from administration of the town's one motorized corn mill.

Arriving at Consensus

As we will see in later pages, there is much factionalism in Ixtepeji, which is increased by a strong individualism of the people. The question that must be asked, then, is: What is it that counteracts these tendencies and insures the continuity of the social organism? We can refer to one such factor as "the enemy that unites."

The presence of nearby communities who have recently been their deadly foes influences Ixtepejanos to have a wary attitude toward the outer world in general. It is in the face of outsiders that the townspeople close ranks and present a solid front. Concern with town unity and the prevention of internal factional disputes that could "divide the town" (*dividir el pueblo*) are strongly expressed themes to which we will return later.

The fact that Ixtepeji is unique in the Sierra Juárez for having been a camp of "rebels" surrounded by enemies is no doubt in part an explanation for one of its most remarkable social features, namely its *asambleas* or town meetings. Other towns in the area have asambleas, but Ixtepeji's are renowned for the fact that the entire adult male community actually comes together and arrives at decisions by a fundamentally democratic process. There are two types of assemblies, *ordinarias* (*asambleas de consejo*) and *generales*. The ordinarias are attended by the ayuntamiento, the *Junta Vecina*, and the *Comité Educativo*. They usually meet once each month to arrange for minor community and school *fiestas*, to handle matters pertaining to the community corn mill, and so forth. The more important *asambleas generales* are held according to necessity, as well as at regular intervals for elections. Their main function is to decide on community projects and assess the labor and taxes necessary, to elect cargo holders, and to make any other major decisions that involve the town or municipio as a whole. Custom requires every male in the town of cargo serving age to attend plus representatives from the agencias. There is a five peso fine for the first asamblea missed and ten pesos for each successive absence. Being away from the area, however, is a valid excuse for absence. Ixtepejanos are quick to point out, and truly, that at these meetings everyone has the right to speak, either to back someone else, or to criticize, or just to state an opinion.

In November 1966 the most important asamblea general of the year was held to take care of general matters and to fill the one-year cargos for the following year. It followed the meetings of the barrios, and was attended by about 130 men. It started about 6:30 P.M. following a three or four hour interval after the barrio meetings broke up. Most men spent this time hanging around the *tienditas*, drinking and talking in small groups scattered around the municipio area. When it got started, men began to crowd into the room, most of them sitting on timbers arranged in rows on the floor for this purpose. The meeting began with a reading of the list of adult male citizens over the public address system with the loud-speaker placed outside in the patio so that it is heard out in the town. Inside, each man answered with a *presente* to his name. The main order of business was the announcement of the selections made by the barrios and the election of the annual municipio cargos. This latter proceeds in the following pattern rather consistently: Someone will propose the name of so-and-so for the cargo; if present the nominee will decline, arguing that he has not had enough "rest" since his last cargo or sufficient experience or is not going to be in town. Then follows a discussion of these points and clarification of how much "rest" he has had and what other cargos he has fulfilled. Then someone will either propose that they take his objection into consideration or they vote to elect him. In almost all instances, the latter was the case and the person was "elected" by a show of hands, which is virtually always unanimous, no vote to the contrary ever being taken. In all cases except the election of the alcalde only one candidate was nominated and elected; for the alcalde, three candidates were nominated according to a formality, although it was understood that the first nomination was the one to be elected and the only one anyone was to vote for, excepting the nominators of the other two candidates.

In only a few instances did the nominated candidate acknowledge that he was ready and willing to accept the cargo. This was immediately answered with a round of applause and cheering. In cases where nominated candidates declined and the ensuing discussion led to a vote, the mood of the voting was like a crowd of Romans giving a thumbs-down decision in the Colosseum—much joking and laughter and an explosion of hands when the vote was called for, occasionally punctuated with shouts of *todos, todo el pueblo.*

Several absent men were named to various cargos after it was ascertained that they had had at least two years of "rest." In several instances where young men attempted to decline their first or second cargo for reasons of inexperience, the presidente or some other older man would coax them, arguing that it was good for them to start their cargos early so they could pass through (*escalar*) them and get them over with before they were old men. Also chosen by this all male group were the officers of the *Liga Femenil.* The procedure was the same as for the other cargos, except that fathers and brothers of the women nominated accepted or attempted to decline the cargos for them, *viz.*, women had no apparent say on their destinies in these matters. In the selections made at the barrio meetings, it is understood that the old men will decide what cargos the younger men appointed for these offices will hold; there is no voting there. At about 10 P.M. someone proposed that they stop to allow everyone to go home and eat; this was emphatically voted down and the presidente ordered the policía not to let anyone leave, although men were free to go out to the patio to urinate. The presidente did grant a request for the men from the agencias to go out for dinner since most of them had missed it. The asamblea finally stopped past 3 A.M. with several items of business left, which were continued the next day.

Barrio Organization

According to legend the five barrios of Ixtepeji were formed from five different local Zapotec settlements that the Spanish concentrated in the sixteenth century at the present location of Ixtepeji. This event is referred to as the congregación. Those moved into the *congregación* from what is now the site of the agencia of San Pedro Nexicho (Zapotec: *Netxicho*, people of the *rincón*) were originally from the rincón area to the east, and formed barrio San Pedro. People previously living near the ruins of the chapel of Ziigu (Zapotec: *ziigu*, the old ones) which was the first settlement in the area formed barrio San Juan Evangelista. Barrio San Juan Bautista was formed from a settlement on the Cerro de las Salinas. And, those living on the hill between town and San Pedro where the ruins are, became barrio San Nicolás. An original settlement on the site of the present town became barrio San Miguel. Until the time of the town's destruction, the barrios remained localized, each one occupying a certain part of the town delimited by definite boundaries. Old informants say that barrio exogamy was a prescribed rule that was usually followed. When the survivors returned, however, to resettle in 1921, the destruction and natural weathering away of houses and overgrowth of vegetation was so extensive that they established new house sites where they could. They did, however, retain former barrio affiliation, so that the result today is that the five original topographic barrios are scrambled. Barrio membership is no longer a factor in marriage selection, but a woman does adopt the barrio membership of her husband, and children assume the barrio membership of their father.

The previous section mentioned how the barrios contribute to the formal structure of the town's religious and civil hierarchies. Another significant event in which the individual barrios draw together and express solidarity is the fiesta of their patron saint. On this day, once a year, the "sons of the barrios" come together for a day of feasting, drinking, and speech making to reaffirm their unity and brotherhood. These events provide one more opportunity for individuals to host their neighbors and demonstrate their good will to them. The trappings are religious; that is, the image of the patron is conveyed to and from the fiesta site in a procession and the priest's benedictions are paid for, if he is available. But otherwise, the content of speeches and the nature of interpersonal relations are not different from fiestas in general. As with other such occasions, these are primarily male events, which they organize and in which they are the main participants, women and children being peripheral spectators who join in the processions and activities in the church.

At present the barrio system seems to be straining. People recognize that there is a growing disproportion in size such that Barrio San Juan Bautista is the largest, while San Nicolás and San Juan Evangelista are much smaller and shrinking. This is already reflected in their differential representation in the civil and religious hierarchies. There are some informants who speculate that it will not be long before the barrio system as it is now will collapse due to this growing disproportion. But there are theoretical reasons to believe that it will evolve into a stable two barrio system. There is already good evidence that such a process is well underway and has been for some time. For, at present, there is a well established informal opposition that cleaves the town into two approximately equal halves referred to as "up and down." There is general agreement that "those from below and those from above" are separated by a single street that runs horizontally across the general vertical slope of the town, although those who live near this boundary are apt to be less emphatic in specifying the division precisely. Thus, although up–down membership is not as exactly specified as in the case of formal barrio membership, and although the up–down division becomes fuzzy on the edges of town and near this horizontal division, the important thing is that everyone is well aware of the distinction and makes frequent reference to it.

In general, this up–down division is not basically different from the type of opposition reported from other Mesoamerican two-barrio towns. I myself first became aware of it when I noticed that several informants asked me if the people from "down there" or "up there" ever spoke to me or were friendly to me, and also if it were not true that the people of their respective areas were not more friendly. In general, the epithets applied to the up's and down's by each other are the same; for example, they are more egotistical, niggardly, miserly, closed and stupid. Although women are well aware of the opposition, they are less dramatic and forceful in their expression of it than males for whom it is a more significant reality, especially boys and young men. The opposition has been known to exist at least since the resettlement of the town from which time there has been an ongoing history of fighting and minor feuding between youths of the two sections. The most common event that precipitates such occurrences is when an individual from one side, alone or accompanied by a friend, invades the other side to visit or serenade a girl. Consistent with this is the recognition that marriages are more frequent across the up–down boundary than within either side. This opposition becomes a real thing early in the life of small boys who are often made painfully aware of it by being stoned by youths from the other side when they have to enter into it for various reasons.

Looking for causes for the geographical orientation of this opposition, most possibilities are soon eliminated. There is no appreciable wealth or other social differences between the up's and the down's. Furthermore, because of the tendency to intermarriage, the two halves of the town are linked together by a continuous web of kinship. Nor is there any basis for the opposition resulting from the formal barrio structure. However, one physical feature of the town that appears to be at least indirectly related to this is the system of water distribution. The town's water supply comes by the above mentioned canal. After it enters the town, it runs along the hillside above the center of the town and gives off seven parallel canals which run down through the town. Individual lots are watered by smaller side ditches. In the dry season, water is always scarce and irrigation is regulated according to a list maintained in the municipio, which indicates when individuals may divert water into their land. This system is cause for many disputes that arise when someone higher on one of the lateral canals diverts water during someone else's appointed time. Since the water flows from top to bottom, those at the upper end are in a preferred position for access to water or, looking at it from another point of view, of having less chance of their water being cut off by uncooperative neighbors. Water disputes are one of the most common causes of complaint brought to the ayuntamiento. When a person believes his water to have been unjustly cut off, he may directly approach the offending party or make a complaint against him to either the presidente or síndico, both of whom have equal authority to impose a fine of from twenty to thirty pesos if they find the accusation to be correct. Obviously, this type of dispute does not divide the town into the distinct halves and even causes many disputes among the up's and down's themselves. But what it does do is to orient this particular type of conflict along a vertical dimension. It may even have been the initial cause of it, but one thing that is certain is that it reinforces it.

Intercommunity Relations

An incident that happened to me once north of Oaxaca City demonstrates the way the people of Ixtepeji see their town in relation to neighboring towns. I cite this incident since it sums up the expression of the quality of intercommunity relations in the Sierra, which are quite similar. Driving south on the Pan American Highway, near Amatitlán, I gave a ride to a young man about twenty-six years old. He was going to Huajuapan. He had just drunk a lot, and got progressively drunker as we went along. He spoke haltingly about his work at the new cement factory near Amatitlán, the condition of the road, and other trivia until we passed through Acatlán. Here he became vehement and began to speak of the "bad people, the brutes that live there," and repeatedly called them killers, saying that they liked to kill people for no reason, "they just pull out their pistols and kill," and also that they all carried knives that they used with the same vengeance. While delivering these intermittent cathartic tirades, interspersed with moments of morose silence, he dramatically demonstrated gun shot wounds and stabbings with gestures and sounds. He occasionally also made more contemplative comments to the effect that things should not be so, that "all have the right to live, all have the right to eat, drink, and work, but not the right to kill." Further down the road, on passing Petalcingo, he essentially repeated the same performance somewhat less energetically, but similarly equating the people of Petalcingo with those of Acatlán. Pulling into Huajuapan where he lives I asked him, "and how are the people here?" He replied, "They are very good people. Here there is no danger, it is very peaceful."

Such an outpouring of emotions and ideas about neighboring towns, although not usually this strongly expressed, is often evoked when speaking with informants about other nearby towns, especially Ixtlán. Once while I was talking with old Pedro Ruiz about the past of Ixtlán, he waved his hand in the direction of Ixtlán, contemptuously spat on the ground and said, "Ixtlán has no history, it has only filthy politicians, it has a shameful history." It has been bitter for Ixtepejanos to have watched the relative fortunes of Ixtepeji and Ixtlán reversed in the last few generations. Ixtlán is now about twice as large as Ixtepeji and more prosperous, due in part to its being located on the new road and its proximity to the mines in Natividad, which are still operating. And as ever, Ixtepejanos are still under the official jurisdiction of their rival and have to submit to other such humiliations as being summoned there for meetings, sending topiles there on foot to collect their mail, and being further down the scale of regional political patronage.

With the exception of Ixtlán, there is today fairly regular though limited trading, contracting of labor, exchange of bands at fiestas, and participation in basketball tournaments between Ixtepeji and her neighbors, although economic relations are much stronger with towns of the rincón. Speaking with informants about such matters, one is apt to get quite a different impression of how they perceive intercommunity relations with nearby towns, for they often emphasize how the entire Sierra is united into one large system of friendly towns. At first such speech seemed quite paradoxical when compared to the impressions conveyed about neighboring towns in other talks, until I realized that this evaluation is dependent on the context in which it is made. I first became aware of this while talking one morning with old Faustino Acevedo. He wanted to know, asking me more or less rhetorically, if I as an outsider ever had any problems when traveling around in the Sierra. I said no and he proceeded to explain how safe travel in the Sierra is, but that the Valley of Oaxaca is a different matter. "There, all the towns around Oaxaca are full of murderers and thieves who will kill a stranger in the night if they think he has money in his pocket. But here an outsider can come into town, get drunk and fall down in the street and most likely someone will go out and bring him into their house and send him on his way in the morning."

What he was saying was that in spite of the old animosities between Ixtepeji and her neighbors, there is still one thing that tends to bind them all together and this is being serranos. But it is not so much being serranos per se that is significant, but being serranos as opposed to people of the Valley. There is in effect a rather sharp line that separates the "bad people" of the valley from the "good people" of the Sierra, which runs where the steep ascent into the mountains begins. This age old and perhaps universal opposition between mountain people and those of the lowlands is also expressed in a preference for the climate, the geography, and general setting as well; the Sierra is said to be healthier and easier to survive in and so forth. But mainly sociological factors are expressed as being the basis of the difference. For example, Emilio León and Pascual Ramírez were once talking at great length about how backward and closed the towns of the Sierra were, especially those that speak much Zapotec. But they then proceeded to contrast it with the Valley in general. "The Valley is full of killers. But around here in the Sierra there are only good people; you can go anywhere with four or five loaded animals without danger. Of course you are armed, but that's only for little things." Similarly, Raul Ruiz once told me, "The people of the Valley are more closemouthed, and very unfriendly. If you oppose them at all, they attack you with machetes or guns. It's more dangerous there than here. Here the people are very peaceful."

The towns nearby are often seen as enemy territory but, if when you go there you watch your step and deal only with those you know you will be all right. Otherwise, they are not too different from people in Ixtepeji, having essentially the same customs and way of life. But, to venture out of the Sierra is to go into foreign territory where a serrano is disadvantaged because of his relative lack of sophistication and his distance from help in case of need.

3

Town History and Myth

L OOKING TO THE HISTORIC PAST for explanations of the present is always an uncertain endeavor. However, in examining the conditions through which Ixtepeji world view and society evolved, several dominant themes emerge that make them more understandable as they are today. On one hand this task is made easy, since events of the past were often so deeply impressed into the minds, institutions, and countryside of the people, that the scars are still visible and their effects on the present readily discernible. On the other hand, time and memories have not been accurate recorders of events, which have been forgotten or, as is more often the case, have become the raw material of a rich mythogenesis—an interesting problem in itself that we will examine.

In unraveling the recent past of Ixtepeji—roughly the period within this century—two very different accounts of the same events are given, which vary with respect to moral pronouncements made on the people and groups involved. We might refer to one as the "official history," that is, the accounts that one finds in the writings of scholars and historians, as well as the yellow newspapers of the state archives. The other version is the one told by the people "who lived through it and saw it with their own eyes." These are the old people of the area, many of whom graciously spent many long hours talking with me, so that I would be sure to get "the true history." And also, much is drawn from the younger adults who have learned from their parents. In reconstructing the "official history" I have relied heavily on the writings of and personal discussions with the state historian of Oaxaca, Dr. Jorge Fernando Iturribarría. I have also drawn from the Cuadros Sinópticos (1883) of the Oaxaca State Library, Padre Gay (1950), Pérez García (1956), and other primary and secondary sources. After presenting this historical sketch we may contrast it with materials collected from self-appointed chroniclers of the town and attempt to explain the differences that arise.

Pre-Columbian Period

Although there is little written history of Ixtepeji, unexcavated terraced hilltop ruins on the outskirts of the town testify to the antiquity of settlement in the area. What is known about the early history of Ixtepeji comes from a document written in 1579 by the magistrate (*corregidor*) Juan Jiménez Ortiz upon request of the Viceroy of New Spain, Martín Enríquez. According to this account the original settlers of Ixtepeji came from the area around Yolox in the Chinatec region to the northeast, between 650 and 700 A.D. They were led there by a chief known as Gualao-Tzotzi-Quetz, or Captain of the War. Two other groups from the same area settled nearby, one of them founding the town of San Miguel del Río. Eventually these three communities formed a short-lived military confederation with other communities, including Teococuilco, Zaachila, Cuilapan, Oaxaca, and Zooquiapan, and strengthened their bonds by exchanging women in marriage.

Throughout the following centuries these people were subjugated at various times by the Mixtecs from Oaxaca and the Aztecs from the Central Highlands, both of whom extracted tribute from them, which consisted of gold, bird plumes, deer, turkeys, firewood, and corn. The Aztecs also forced them to do private work for their personnel in Oaxaca. In order to obtain the gold and feathers to fulfill these obligations, Ixtepejanos traveled to the Isthmus of Tehuantepec and to Guatemala, hiring themselves out as cargo bearers, and often remaining there as laborers for six to eight months.

Jiménez Ortiz reports that the Ixtepejanos venerated a small oracular stone idol, which they adorned with green feathers, but for which they had no special priests. They worshiped it by carrying it to temples on hill tops, where they mortified themselves before it by cutting or piercing their ears, noses, and tongues. They then offered their blood to the idol; those who could not spare the blood due to sickness sacrificed turkeys or dogs and washed the idol with their blood instead. The greater the quantity of blood, the greater the value the sacrifice was considered to have.

Marriage customs seem to have been similar to those of today. The youth asked permission of the bride's family, and if it was not granted the bride might be abducted for several days and then brought to reside in the home of the groom's parents. At this time she was also taken to the idol where a fiesta and drunkenness ensued. Also, as exists today, there seems to have been a definite double standard in that adultery by women was strongly sanctioned against and provided cause for a husband to return his wife to her family, which in turn was considered as a great affront.

The pre-Columbian Ixtepejanos seem to have been involved in states of more or less constant warfare with some of the same settlements with which they have fought in this century. According to Jiménez Ortiz they fought for no special reasons and at times apparently for pure sport, preferably with the nearby settlements of Zooquiapan, Chicomezúchil, Teococuilco, Cuilapan, and also Chinatec towns. Jiménez Ortiz also reports that the first prisoner taken in battle was sacrificed to the idol by ripping out his heart, smearing his blood on the idol, and then ritually cannibalizing him.

Colonial and Post-Colonial Periods

The Ixtepejanos first heard of the arrival of the Spaniards in Vera Cruz from the people of Cuilapan who told them that the sea had thrown up some men dressed in iron who were said to be children of the sun. An old manuscript, which for years was stored in the archives of the municipio, relates that Cortés invited the Ixtepejanos to join him in fighting the Aztecs. The leader of the Ixtepejanos was at this time a *cacique* known as Coquelay who accepted the request and marched with Cortés to the Aztec capital of Tenochtitlán with some 200 Ixtepejanos, all but twenty of whom perished on the shores of the surrounding lakes. As a reward for helping to put him on the throne of Montezuma, Cortés gave the title of "Cacique of the Forty Towns" to the son of Coquelay and baptized him Juan Juárez de Zárate. Within two years the Spaniards had penetrated into the Valley of Oaxaca, and the people of Cuilapan called upon the Ixtepejanos to help repulse the invaders. At the end of the ensuing campaigns Ixtepeji was subjugated under the authority of the *encomendero* Pedro Aragonés, who after fifteen years was succeeded by his son Juan de Arágon, upon whose death in 1536 the custody of the town came under the authority of the corregidores. Jiménez Ortiz also reports that there were severe epidemics in 1540 and 1567 that reduced the population to a mere 160 individuals. In 1565 the site of the town was officially established at the present location; this was the formal *congregación* of the community for the purpose of more effective conversion to Catholicism and extraction of tribute, both of which the people resisted by persistently attempting to retreat further back into the mountains.

In the mid-sixteenth century when Juan de Aragón was the encomendero, Ixtepeji consisted of five *estanzuelas* (today called agencias or ranchos). There is a record that indicates that there were 451 *tributarios* (payers of tribute) who delivered the following goods: 37 pesos every 60 days; 6 chickens daily; 400 cacaos, the service of 9 men and 2 women every ten days; and 280 fanegas of corn and 10 fanegas of beans annually. In addition they were required to deliver quantities of salt, honey, and chile. At this time there were no mines, but the climate was appropriate for the cultivation of silk, wheat, and cochineal, which were introduced.

Later, in parts of the seventeenth and eighteenth centuries, Ixtepeji formed part of the dukedom of Atlixco, but little is known of it in this period. In 1660 there was a widespread Indian uprising in Oaxaca, which first broke out in Tehuantepec. Ixtepeji was one major center of the rebellion that was soon put down by the Spanish overlords. From this time through the Revolutionary period the record is full of numerous minor armed conflicts between Ixtepeji and neighboring towns and throughout the Sierra Juárez in general.

It is said that until the first part of this century there was in the municipal archives a codex drawn on deer skin measuring about 7 by 1 meters, which described the boundaries of the territory of Ixtepeji as well as those of adjacent areas in the Valley of Oaxaca. It specified Tlalixtac as *cabecera* of the Valley and Ixtepeji as cabecera of the Sierra. Supposedly, the man who was municipal president from 1908 to 1911 wished to legalize the limits of the town and so delivered the codex to a lawyer in Oaxaca who in turn sold it to the German consul for 35,000 pesos.

This event apparently also figured as one of the causes of the rebellion of the town in 1912.

Twentieth Century

Events in this century in the Sierra Juárez and Oaxaca, which have shaped Ixtepeji as it is today, are only comprehensible within the greater national context. The most significant aspect of this larger milieu is the drama of the Revolution, which began in 1910. The ensuing sixteen years in Oaxaca were ones of almost continual warfare involving virtually the entire population, rural and urban, rich and poor. The chroniclers of this period monotonously repeat recurrent episodes. There were numerous massacres of communities and counter-reprisals, a general economic stagnation and social disintegration of the region, and an absence of any semblance of political stability as allegiances shifted like the wind. Battle fatalities, epidemics, starvation, and emigration caused a large population decline. In the countryside the onerous conditions that weighed down on the peasants during the dictatorship intensified. Although many towns such as Ixtepeji escaped the yoke of *caciques* (political strong men) at this time, the price in death, misery, and destruction was high. The experience of these years has left its mark on the people, their institutions, and world view.

Early and intense opposition in Oaxaca to the Díaz regime resulted in the formation of a Revolutionary Junta, loosely connected with the National Revolutionary Party. Despite strong persecution by the reactionary state government, members of and sympathizers with the Junta continued to organize and agitate in Oaxaca. Soon after the first battles of the Revolution broke out in 1910, in Puebla and Chihuahua, the liberal forces in Oaxaca took up arms against the state, then headed by Díaz's nephew, Felix, whom the old dictator appointed as governor just before stepping down from the presidency. Expectation that Benito Juárez Masa, a prominent member of the Antire-electionist Party and son of Benito Juárez, would be governor added to the opposition to Felix Díaz.

In mid-1910 the clearest lines of opposition were drawn (and this is an oversimplification of a complex situation) between the liberal Maderistas and the conservative old guard that still held considerable political power and patronage in the countryside. In the Sierra Juárez the situation was somewhat different. Isolated as it was by rugged terrain and the absence of roads other than narrow trails, the entire area was effectively cut off from the provincial capital and as such was ruled by local strong men, the most notable of whom were Guillermo Meixuero and his second in command, Onofre Jiménez, both of Ixtlán. Juan Carrasco and Pedro León were the strong men of Ixtepeji, and its nearby agencia of San Pedro Nexicho, respectively. Because of the political strength and conservative basis of the Díaz regime, the strong men of the Sierra found it in their best interests to support it, except Carrasco and León who, because of the vicissitudes of local developments, were soon to commit the people of Ixtepeji to a long and bloody struggle with their neighboring towns. Ixtepejanos make their first appearance in the "official history" at this time in an event that begins the involvement of the Sierra Juárez in the Revolution.

At Xía, not far from Ixtepeji, on the road to Ixtlán, was the site of a large textile mill, operated by workers from Ixtepeji. Here on June 4, 1910, they rose up in armed revolt against the owners. Madero forces and Antimaderistas alike in the neighboring towns of Ixtlán, Jaltianguis, Guelatao, Analco, Yolox, and others, viewed the revolt with fear and organized armed forces to oppose the rebels from Ixtepeji. These events signalled the beginning of open warfare and inestimable suffering and destruction. Iturribarría summarizes the situation as follows: "In effect, once the serranos turned to the use of arms, and in view of the precarious agricultural base of the region, and the resulting closing of the mines and plant at Xía, they could not return to a peaceful life and were thus converted by force of circumstances into active instruments of armed pressure, easily made use of in all the fluctuations of politics and strong man bossism, and later the local movement of·state sovereignty" (Iturribarría 1955:270–271; my translation, as are all of the following).

The state government also responded to the Ixtepejano's action at Xía by recruiting soldiers from the Sierra to suppress them. The general result of this campaign was to convert the people of Ixtepeji from a relatively prosperous town of farmers and traders into an outlaw band of guerrillas.

Meanwhile in the Valley, Juárez was now governor (1911), but was strongly opposed by the *sobernistas*, or proponents of state sovereignty, in contrast to the Ixtepejanos, who became identified with Juárez. Unable to beat the Ixtepejanos by force of arms, Juárez invited them to join him and established the Batallón Sierra Juárez. Juárez appointed Pedro León, leader from the agencia of San Pedro Nexicho, to command the Ixtepejanos. This period of military service under Juárez gave the Ixtepejanos considerable experience in the art of warfare, which they were to practice intensively for the next ten years. In 1912 Juárez died suddenly of an apparent heart attack. Without his protection the Ixtepejanos rightly feared that reprisals would be made against them for atrocities they had committed while in his service, and so one night they surreptitiously abandoned Oaxaca City, taking large quantities of arms and munitions with them. Significant in their decision to return to the Sierra was the rumor that Juárez had been poisoned by enemies who had sworn to deal with the Ixtepejanos. Ixtepejanos still believe this explanation of Juárez's death, although other sources do not support this theory.

By now the events that were shaping the destiny of Ixtepeji, which began with the rebellion at Xía, were growing to monumental and tragic proportions. "After the death of Juárez the deserting brigade dedicated itself to vandalism and terrorism, after having recruited and incorporated into its horde other serranos who were not shy in following them since they too lacked other means to go on living. Thus grew this army without a flag or law until they arrived in a position of attempting an assault on the capital of the state" (*Ibid.* 280). During this time they openly used Ixtepeji as the center for their operations, which one source describes as "roving in search of plunder" (Tamayo 1956:30).

After an unsuccessful five-day siege of Oaxaca City, in which they succeeded in isolating it and causing great loss of life on both sides, the Ixtepejanos broke off the attack and returned to the Sierra, pausing to plunder the town of Huayapan and their old enemy Tlalixtac. Once again in the Sierra they continued to live as robbers, without losing their objective of recruiting more men and returning for another attempt on the capital. Their leader, Pedro León, was angered when Atepec refused to support him, and sent men to take possession of the town. But the Atepecanos overwhelmed and captured them. Angered by this turn of events, León solicited aid from Jaltianguis, which received him as a friend until they were able to overpower his escort and take them all prisoners. "Tied like a ferocious beast, he was taken to the cabecera at Ixtlán and executed there on the tenth of June. His son of the same name wasted no time in taking his place and continuing the misdeeds of his father" (Iturribarría 1955:281–282).

In the following year the Ixtepejanos engaged in several major clashes with government forces that were sent into the Sierra to pacify them. The toll in one of these battles fought at San Juan Chicomezúchil was over 300 killed. In reprisal the Ixtepejano leaders—Juan Carrasco, Pedro Justino León (son of Pedro León), Pedro Jiménez, and Ignacio Castellanos—laid siege to their old rival, Ixtlán, and prevented surrounding towns from carrying supplies into it, hoping in this manner to break the hold of the government forces dug in there. The government forces, unable to withstand the siege, evacuated the town and left it in the hands of the Ixtepejanos. "The Ixtepejanos burned Ixtlán and violated the graveyard to recover the remains of their chief, Pedro León, who was buried there" (*Ibid.* 1955:282). Encouraged by this victory over their old antagonists in Ixtlán, the Ixtepejanos, lusting for another attempt on Oaxaca City, augmented their forces by promising that recruits could take booty from the sacking of the city. But this time the capital was better defended and the Ixtepejanos were routed, leaving behind many dead and wounded. Following this defeat they broke up into several smaller bands and continued to plunder towns in the Valley and the Sierra.

There is little mention of the final defeat of the Ixtepejanos and the destruction of their town, except for a few lines by Iturribarría and by Tamayo. Tamayo best describes the attacks:

> In order to end the revolt it was decided to attack Ixtepeji by sending three converging columns on it from Etla, Tlalixtac, and Tlacolula. The one entering the mountains from Tlalixtac was routed at Los Pozos, but being later reinforced by Issac Ibarra it was able to continue on to Lachatao. The other two columns joined up and attacked Ixtepeji on the eleventh of November. At a critical moment in the battle the column from Etla arrived and attacked from the rear, thus breaking the resistance of the rebels. Eight hundred Ixtepejanos were captured and the town burned. The victorious troops with an absurd rage and cruelty then burned down several other towns in the districts of Villa Alta and Los Cajones (Tamayo 1956: 30).

Later Tamayo passes judgment that, "One cannot hold the Ixtepejanos guilty. Surrounded by local enemies they had no alternative but to take up arms against the Revolution" (*Ibid.* 34). "With the capture of the Serrano–Ixtepejano leaders, Juan Carrasco and Pedro Justino León, and a large group of their followers, the pressure in this part of the state was relieved . . ." (Iturribarría 1955:289).

Most of the captured men of Ixtepeji were impressed into the army and sent to the north where a large contingent of them formed a colony in Chihuahua. Others participated in the battles of Guaymas and Sonora where, led by their own generals Carrasco and León, and the Oaxacan general Luis Figueroa, they fought against Obregon's forces. Other Ixtepejano prisoners were sent to the "Siberia Mexicana" as was then called the inhospitable territory of Quintana Roo. Those who escaped the siege and rape of the town or impressment into the army (mainly older men, women, and children), sought refuge in Oaxaca City or the towns of the *rincón* region to the east where they had traditional ties from trading and family relations.

Exact causes for the intense animosity between Ixtepeji and her neighboring towns, especially Ixtlán, which culminated in the destruction of the town and later mutual blood letting, are not explained solely by political and ideological motives. In seeking to uncover underlying historic roots of this opposition, I arrived at the following hypothesis: In the eighteenth and nineteenth centuries, Ixtepeji had been the commercial and cultural center and largest town of the Sierra due to its mines and location as a trade center. But Ixtlán, which was otherwise less significant than Ixtepeji, had been chosen as the *cabecera*, or governmental center of the district, because of administrative decisions in the colonial period.

The Ixtepejanos were therefore annoyed that they had to take their affairs to their smaller rival. Ixtlán, on the other hand, was envious of Ixtepeji's general good fortune and also wished to acquire some of Ixtepeji's extensive municipal territory, which is the largest in the area. Mutual bad feelings thus arose so that events in the opening days of the Revolution were sufficient to trigger open hostilities.[1]

Other chance circumstances of this period, also quite apart from the popularly expressed political and ideological reasons, determined Ixtepeji's destiny. These too must be understood within the context of the early days of the Revolution. As it happened, at this time pro-Madero and anti-Díaz sentiments prevailed in most of the Sierra. Because of the logic underlying the town's antagonisms, the open conflict between the Ixtepejanos, led by Carrasco and León, and their surrounding enemies resulted in the Ixtepejanos becoming defined as antimaderistas. In the ensuing developments of the Revolution, the Ixtepejanos were to be defined with and aligned with whatever the strong men of the Sierra were against. Thus, in the soon to come resurgence of reactionary powers in the state, culminating in the state sovereignty movement to break away from the Republic, the Ixtepejanos were identified with the constitutionalist forces of President Carranza with whom they fought. As they say in Ixtepeji, "We were the only *brazo carranzisto* in the Sierra."

Meanwhile, in the rest of the state the turmoil of the Revolution took its toll. Although Oaxaca had the good fortune to remain out of the major campaigns, small uprisings and bloody clashes, such as the defeat of Ixtepeji, were endemic. By 1914, general economic distress and plague were scourging not only the country-

---

[1] A similar opposition exists between nearby Yalalag and its economically and culturally less significant *cabecera*, Villa Alta (De La Fuente 1949:253–254). For other local historic conflicts that are still active *cf.* De La Fuente (1949:251–254) and Nader (1964:211–212).

Ixtepejanos who were drafted into the federal army.

Ixtepejano volunteers sent by the federal government to fight in the revolutionary campaigns in northern Mexico.

side but Oaxaca City itself. In this atmosphere, old anticonstitutionalist, state sovereignist enemies of Ixtepeji, led by Meixuero, aligned themselves with the despotic Huerta who was now in power in Mexico. In part, as reward for their role in pacification of rebels in the Sierra in 1912, these forces were given free reign by the federal government to enact their "Plan of the Sierra," which was put into operation by the siege and taking of Oaxaca, thereby deposing the local government, composed mainly of former Madero and Juárez followers. The reactionaries were thus back on top, with Meixuero the power behind the throne. Once again in control, the sovereignists sought to widen the separation of the state from the federal government, now back in the hands of the northern constitutionalists.

The tides of power in Oaxaca soon turned again. In November 1914 a constitutionalist force led by the northern Jiménez Figueroa brothers and reinforced by a group of stray soldiers from Ixtepeji, marched on and captured Oaxaca City. The serrano generals once again retreated from their city houses to their mountain strongholds where they planned counterattacks and reprisals which they carried out in mid-November. The Figueroa forces and some sixty Ixtepejanos chose to defend the city, but were routed. Figueroa and some thirty-five or forty Ixtepejanos escaped to a constitutionalist garrison under the command of General Juan Lechuga in Tehuacán. Now again in the palace of Oaxaca and frustrated in his attempts to wreak vengeance on his old enemies, Meixuero demanded of President Carranza that he deliver Figueroa and the Ixtepejanos to the state to answer for their actions; apparently he also falsely charged them with disloyalty to Carranza. This latter deceit and the military and political vicissitudes of the day induced Carranza to betray the men in Techuacán, ordering Lechuga to remit them to Meixuero in Oaxaca. Upon receiving his orders, Lechuga told Figueroa of his fate and, dismayed by the treachery, allowed Figueroa the chance to run for his life, saying he would be allowed to go free if he escaped the first shots that Lechuga's duty required him to fire. Figueroa took his chances and received a bullet in the back. Figueroa's second in command suffered the same fate. The Ixtepejanos, however, were not afforded such magnanimity and were herded into a special train for Oaxaca, and finally into the hands of Meixuero and his henchmen. Iturribarría best describes the ensuing events:

When the train from Tehuacán arrived at the station of San Antonio Nanahuatipan at the border between Oaxaca and Puebla, the bodies of Figueroa and Cadena were buried in the municipal cemetery.

What occurred in the night of this same day, in the same station, is one of the most repugnant episodes of the epoch and probably has no parallel in the history of Oaxaca: The Ixtepeji soldiers and their officers were herded into a corner and in the midst of ferocious screaming were riddled with bullets, not one of them surviving. Nor did their executioners even bury them, leaving this task to be done by local authorities.

In this manner the serranos settled two accounts: the recent taking of the palace in Oaxaca, and a debt from two years earlier when in 1912 the Ixtepejanos and the citizens of Ixtlán fought each other and turned themselves into irreconcilable enemies (Iturribarría 1955:320–321).

At about this point, Ixtepeji ceases to appear in the "official history." In the ensuing years battles were waged between the sovereignists and constitutionalists, with Oaxaca City changing hands between them several times. During this period the anti-Ixtepeji forces in the Sierra controlled the territory there, and marched into the city when the tides of warfare and politics favored the reactionaries. By 1924, the federal government had stabilized and the sobernista movement in Oaxaca died. This year (1924) marks the beginnings of relative tranquillity in which survivors of the revolution continued to resettle their devastated town and started to heal the old wounds, some of them after walking home from the campaigns in Sonora and Chihuahua. Meanwhile, the entire state continued in a long period of general economic decline and emigration from which it has not yet recovered.

The Myth

We can now leave the recent history of Ixtepeji as it is formally recorded and turn to the accounts of the same period told by townspeople who survived this era. From the events and their interpretations summarized in the preceding pages, we see that the historians do not treat the Ixtepejanos kindly. Nor are such sentiments different from those of many old Oaxacans who lived through the period when the rebels were running loose. In neighboring towns one is certain to arouse even stronger emotions by mentioning the events of these bloody years. Although there are other causes for this opposition, memories of the first few years of the Revolution figure strongly. The burden of bearing a villainous reputation cannot but have some effect on the survivors of Ixtepeji's blackest days and their children. And it is this more than anything else that must be kept in mind when interpreting their versions of these years. Their version differs from the official one not so much in details such as events, dates, persons, and places as it does in the interpretations of the motives and morality of people involved. But there is another type of variance between the official history and that of the Ixtepejanos, and this is due to the selective deletion of certain important episodes of the entire narrative. As might be guessed, these are the darker chapters that appear in the official accounts. To say that there is a sense of group guilt about certain of these infamous episodes is to make a premature judgment about the Ixtepeji personality. For the time being it is better just to say that there are whole segments of their recent history that Ixtepejanos do not care to talk about and which they do not readily tell their children. For example, there is old Lisandro who carries a withered arm inside his shirt, a result of a wound from "the time of the Revolution"; any further inquiries about this subject are answered with an abrupt change of topic. Who knows what secret memories he and many of his contemporaries carry? Only one thing is certain —they would rather leave them unspoken.

But this is not to say that there is no concern with history. On the contrary, the people of Ixtepeji have a strong sense of history, and there are many older men who are ready to tell "the true story of the town." I also recorded other versions in neighboring towns and in Oaxaca City. But at no time did I ever directly counter an Ixtepeji informant's narrative with a suggestion that he might be telling things other than as they were. To have done so would have shown great impropriety, but what is more it would have been the cause not only of embarrassment but of a painful recollection of something not wanted to be remembered. Further, in the minds of some informants I am certain that myth has become reality, that the past has been vindicated.

This leads us to the problem of how to account for the discrepancies. The answer has already been partly suggested above; history is used, even altered, to heal the wounds of the past. As we shall see from the following data, there is good reason to assume that this is the case. But what other function can the Ixtepeji versions serve? Leach's criticism and reapplication of traditional functional approach to mythology suggests an answer. Mythology, according to Leach, functions to perpetuate what might be referred to as idealized social structures—that is, structural forms that are not actually extant but that are desirable from the point of view of certain segments of a population. Thus, while Malinowski sees myth and ritual as a charter for what is, Leach sees myth as an instrument used intentionally to promote social change, a weapon used to further desired social forms (Leach 1954:264–278). One of the other functions that traditional functionalists attributed to myth was an inept recording of history. "Where they found inconsistencies in the record, they felt justified in selecting that version which seemed mostly likely to be 'true' or even in inventing parts of the story which appeared to be missing" (*Ibid.* 1954:267). Leach argues that rather than resulting from bad history these inconsistencies are attempts to effect, in the present, changes that are highly valued by virtue of their nonexistence, and made more desirous by the prevalence of conditions contrary to them. The remainder of this section presents some narratives from informants speaking about historical events. In later sections the same themes running through these accounts recur in different contexts. Chapter 12, in particular, contrasts the idealized moral order with social reality and analyzes the relation between them.

What follows is a composite of recent town history compiled from conversations mainly with five individuals, two men and a woman, in their early seventies, and two younger men who have a special interest in town history. In these narratives several things are noticeable. First, there is virtually a complete lack of comment on the years 1910 and 1911, during which time the rebels were on the rampage. In contrast, there is a great concern with the events of 1912, which culminated in the destruction and rape of the town, the massacre and dispersal of the population, and the impressment of surviving men into the army. There is much emphasis here on the suffering and on the ensuing exile of the people. Two other themes are also emphasized: one is the brotherhood, unity, and honor of the townspeople; the other is the enmity and ruthlessness of the surrounding towns whose base motives are given as explanations for the fate inflicted on Ixtepeji.

The trouble all started in 1912 when Juan Carrasco was town president and Pedro León was running things over in San Pedro Nexicho. At this time there was a group of about twelve bandits led by their chief, Miguel Juárez, all of whom were

Ruins of building destroyed during Revolution—in a milpa.

from here, Ixtepeji. But they were traitors to the people whom they robbed and murdered without mercy. They were so ruthless and greedy that they killed cattle of their neighbors often taking only the tongues and hides. Carrasco repeatedly asked the authorities in Ixtlán for help, but since these political bosses were all friends of Miguel Juárez, they did nothing. Finally, things got so bad here that Carrasco took things into his own hands, captured the bandits, killed them, and burned their bodies in the middle of town. When the judge in Ixtlán heard of this, he and the other authorities from there came to arrest Carrasco. But the people of Ixtepeji were expecting this and ambushed them at Xía, killing them all. This was a good thing; they were all corrupt. Things would have been alright, but the enemies of the Revolution in Oaxaca had poisoned Benito Juárez Maza. Since Carrasco and the people of Ixtepeji were the only ones in the Sierra who remained loyal to the Revolution, the traitors in Oaxaca sent the army against us. When the army entered the Sierra, the enemy towns joined in the attack, especially Ixtlán, Lachatao, Latuvi, San Miguel del Río, Amatlán, Atepec, Calpulapan, Analco, San Juan Chicomezúchil, and Tlalixtac de Cabrera in the valley. After the first attacks in which the army shelled the town with cannons on the hills and also killed many people with small arms, there was a trick (*engaño*). They sent a traitor that the people thought they could trust. His message was that the Ixtepejanos were to come to Las Animas for a parley with the government generals. But when the men arrived the enemies surrounded them. After this they captured the rest of the men who were not killed, and marched them off to the army. They were sent away into exile. In the meantime the people from the enemy towns looted and burned the town, and chased the old men, women, and children away except for the women they captured and took with them as slaves. Those who escaped had to live in the mountains like wild animals.

When the captive men were marched through Tlalixtac, where many of them were held before being consigned to the north, they were met with cries of "Death to the Ixtepejanos!" But when they were marched through the streets of Oaxaca City women and girls climbed onto roof tops and balconies where they cried to see the sad plight of these poor men, and threw flowers of benediction down to them. There in Oaxaca City they were herded into the barracks and dungeons like animals before being shipped to Mexico where they were kept in equally bad conditions. [Sebastion Acevedo, for example, gives very dramatic accounts of how he was captured and taken to Oaxaca City to be executed, and then held in a dark dungeon for ninety days. Finally, almost blind and starved to death, he was released and sent to the North to experience more suffering in the battles there.]

Before the battle of Ixtepeji the town was very rich and beautiful, but after the attack, in which about half of the men were killed and the other half captured, there was no one to defend it. The church, which was the first one built in the Sierra, was magnificent, comparable to Santo Domingo in Oaxaca, but the enemies robbed and desecrated it along with everything else. The beautiful church rectory with its large corridors and stone columns, was destroyed along with the municipal building. They took a special solid gold chalice decorated with precious jewels from the church and the army melted down some of the bells for cannon. There is a bell still in San Miguel and Latuvi has another. There are also still many *metates* and other things from here with identifying marks on them in San Miguel. The people of Lachatao took, among other things, the image of the town's patron saint, Santa Catarina, and still have her and some other saints. A special harmonium, which was new at the time, was taken to Ixtlán and is still in the church there. But worst of all was the stealing of a miraculous Christ by the people of Ixtlán. Before the destruction there were many magnificent fiestas and the streets were lined with beautiful houses whose ruins you can still see. These fine homes were left for the looters, full of riches and the fruits of the harvest, when the people were exiled.

Another figure who emerges with nearly the same mythical significance as Carrasco is Delfino León Avendaño, who was captured by the Meixuero forces in Ixtlán just prior to the destruction of the town and was executed there along with three other Ixtepejanos. According to the story, at his execution he pulled his bandana from around his neck and threw it to the people saying to take it as a souvenir of him. He also pulled 100 pesos in silver from his pocket and threw these to them as well, telling them to drink in his name, and finally, he swore that the people of Ixtepeji would someday avenge him.

Recent History

Many informants are quick to point out that Ixtepeji is in many ways a new town, especially that it is now much poorer. The mines and textile mill at Xía have never reopened and the population has only recently returned to what it was in 1912, although the land is less fertile and consequently less able to support it. Since resettlement, the road through the Sierra has been opened where there was previously only a trail. But, whereas the trail that was the main route into the mountains went through Ixtepeji, the new road bypasses it at El Cerezal. It does, however, go directly into Ixtlán, and has been largely responsible for Ixtlán's growing prosperity and ascendancy over Ixtepeji. Although few people are able to express it directly, it seems that the personality of the town has changed also. It is as though the years of war and suffering have left their mark, have reduced a former pride and security. For example, in 1924, less than three years after the resettlement, General García Vigil came with troops to recruit men to fight against reactionary forces in Oaxaca, but he was not greeted by the former bellicose Ixtepejanos ready to go to war once more. His arrival terrified the townspeople who feared that the former conflicts were going to break out again. However, many men were taken away by force and participated in the fighting in Oaxaca City; a number of them were even killed. García Vigil did win this battle, and for once Ixtepeji was on the winning side. But it happened that Ixtlán was with the enemy and thus the animosity between the two towns was kept alive.

In discussing recent events such as these, Ixtepejanos emphasize the terrors of war, their desire for the security of peace and tranquillity, and their fear of both internal and external conflicts. This desire for internal unity and solidarity is strongly emphasized, and Ixtepejanos say it should be maintained at whatever cost. For example, during the last fifteen years or so Ixtepeji has become continually more affiliated with PRI (Institutional Revolutionary Party) headquarters in Oaxaca, the local arm of the monolithic ruling party of the federal government, which has an effective political machine operating at all national levels down to and including the rural villages. Men of responsibility in the town readily stress how the entire town is *priísta*, and that there is no internal division because, "the town doesn't want to be against the government since all the trouble of 1912 started because of such opposition, and we want no more war." It soon becomes apparent, however, and some informants actually say so themselves, that the politics and ideology of PRI are irrelevant, that what is important is to be solidly united with the government and not allow anything to disrupt this unity, that is, to ensure that the entire town presents "a single front." This unity is preserved at the expense of town autonomy, since PRI headquarters has the power to approve municipal elections, so that "the town cannot always dispose as it wishes." But the resulting tranquillity is seen as worth the cost, a point that is demonstrated by referring to conditions in Ixtlán, which is split into political factions that have been fighting each other for years.

There is another event out of recent history that townspeople point to as an object lesson in these matters. In 1936, the town president, Juan Rodríguez Pérez, decided to go further in politics. At this time there was a man of humble origin named Benito Zaragoza from San Antonio Socorro who decided to run for governor against the government candidate Colonel Constantino Chapital. Zaragoza attracted a large backing from rural Oaxaca, including many towns in the Sierra. There were, however, only about twelve men in Ixtepeji besides Rodríguez who were in favor of Zaragoza, "since the town had learned what happens from being against the government." There was much opposition and some armed fighting between the parties before the elections. Rodríguez tried to persuade his fellow Ixtepejanos to support Zaragoza but, with the exception of those original few, they wanted no part of it. He then took it upon himself to sign documents affirming that the entire town was *Zaragozista*, and he even went so far as to arrange with the Zaragoza faction in Lachatao and some other towns to join in an attack on Chapital. The plan was as follows. Rodríguez's friends from Lachatao were to come to Ixtepeji and join forces with the men Rodríguez was to have gathered, and then they were to ambush Chapital when he passed by en route to a political convention in Ixtlán. But because the Ixtepejanos did not go along with him, he could not organize accomplices. Therefore, when the men from Lachatao arrived, they called off the ambush. As a moral footnote, this story ends with the observation that because of this, conditions remained peaceful in Ixtepeji, but Rodríguez, who continued to mix in politics, was killed three years later in Oaxaca City, whether by friends or enemies nobody knows.

4

World View in Ixtepeji

ONTEMPORARY ANTHROPOLOGY has relatively good methods and theories
to handle the more empirically accessible types of behavior such as social
organization, law and politics, language, and ritual, but it is still in the
exploratory stages of the study of abstract systems such as beliefs and values. Progress in this second area is perhaps best made when closely connected with the first.
As Firth has said, the study of values is best done when specifically linked to analysis of social structure. Another aspect of the above distinction is that some anthropologists tend to see behavior as formal structure whereas others, usually more
psychologically oriented, see it in terms of motivation. The aim of this study is
to get at underlying motivation and, at the same time, to establish it within structural contexts. This combined approach is inherent in the concept of "value" (cf.
Kluckhohn 1951). The assumption here is that human social behavior is essentially
choice-making behavior; in other words, for any given human activity there are
always alternative means, modes, and ends of action. Stated as such, the problem
for the anthropologist is to explain why certain means, modes, and ends of action
are taken and not others. Eschewing deterministic and reductionistic arguments,
we can say that selection from among such alternatives are made on the basis of
ideas of what is most positive, for example, on the basis of values. Such choice-
making behavior can of course be done only within the context of existing structures, the social, cultural, and geographical milieux in which they occur. This has
the following theoretical implications. If we assume that choices, and therefore
structures, are dependent on values, we must ask, "How do the values derive?" Since
values must exist within cultural, social, and geographic contexts, or what are better
called environments, they ultimately depend upon the perception of these environments. That is, in order to understand the origin, maintenance, and changes in
values, perception of reality must be understood, the way in which the world is
seen, or simply "world view." Bohannan goes to the crux of the issue by saying,
"Social scientists can afford to beg the question of the nature of reality because it
is perception alone with which they deal" (1963:32).

43

The primary problem thus becomes defining perceptions of the world that we assume to exist in varying degrees of overtness and covertness in the minds of informants, and upon which they base their actions. A series of statements describing the Ixtepeji view of the world appears below, and is referred to as basic, or "existential propositions" (cf. Albert 1956). Historically, derivation of such statements is within one mainstream of American anthropology that has sought to describe cultures in terms of logically interrelated covert assumptions those cultures make about the world. Significant here are Sapir's "unconscious systems of meanings," Hoebel's "postulates," Kluckhohn's "configurations" and "enthymemes," Opler's "cultural themes," Kardiner's "basic personality structure," Hallowell's "basic orientations," Gillin's "ethos components" and the concept of "variations in value-orientations" developed by the Kluckhohns, et al.

What is the nature of such propositions and how are they discovered? Maquet defines this kind of statement as, "a logical inference drawn from observed facts by an anthropologist. . . . It belongs to the theoretical level of anthropology; 'it asserts more than observation gives, and it is not verified directly. . . .' It cannot be said to be true or false; it is a tool which is useful or not" (Maquet 1964:21).

Basic Propositions

1. The world (local, social, and geographic environment) is filled with omnipresent, unknown, and unknowable dangerous beings and entities (natural and supernatural) that constantly threaten the individual. Friends, relatives, strangers, spirits, and natural phenomena are seen as actually or potentially dangerous, and not to be relied on in time of need. The individual is essentially alone in a hostile world in which nothing is secure. Intimates such as friends and relatives, and strangers are potentially the most dangerous.

2. Human and supernatural aggression are performed through deceit and deception. Aggressors attack victims by causing them to lower their defenses. This is done by appearing as someone or something the victim should be able to trust. Appearances, therefore, cannot be trusted because they may be a trap to fool an unwary victim who has let down his defenses. Man, to defend himself, must constantly test appearances; this is easier with material things than abstract things. Material objects are therefore intrinsically more valuable than abstractions (ideas and ideals). Much of what one encounters, especially when it is desirable, is an illusion.

3. Human beings are very susceptible to frustration and are envious of others; both frustration and envy make one wish to harm others. A person who is deprived of something wishes to retaliate by injuring and depriving others who are more fortunate. This desire to retaliate is one of the main motivations in interpersonal relations. It is therefore dangerous to make other people envious since to do so is to make them potential enemies. Also, it is very dangerous to appear envious or discontent since you will then be defined as an enemy. A possible enemy's disposition can be determined by close observation, but this kind of behavior is also dangerous because the person you are observing may misconstrue your attention as a gathering of information for an attack on him. Man acts to guard against the threats of others. Limiting involvement with them to an absolute minimum is the best defense. Cooperation for defense, but not mutual benefit, is maximum safe involvement. A balance must therefore be struck between necessary involvement and protective noninvolvement.

4. *Any change in the status quo will most likely be for the worse; in general things are changing for the worse.* Several attitudes follow from this temporal orientation: The new and the strange are dangerous and threatening. Also, since things tend toward the worst and since the future is unknowable, opportunities and resources should be exploited to the fullest in the present.

5. *Hard work and suffering are inevitable consequences of life.* Life is a struggle; it is something to be borne as an imposed obligation. A person's position in life is determined by fate so that he can improve his life's condition only within the limits set by his destiny; beyond this all personal effort is inconsequential. Within these limits luck and patrons are needed. Since personal control and prevention of undesirable events are not possible, it is most important to be able to endure them.

The next five chapters each discuss one of these five basic propositions. Chapter 5 looks at the concepts of *aire* and *susto*, an important set of folk beliefs and associated practices, and explains it in terms of proposition number 1. Chapter 6 discusses interpersonal relations and some attitudes about the world, in accord with proposition number 2. Chapter 7, elaborating on proposition number 3, continues analyzing the quality of interpersonal relations and related folk concepts of human nature and human motivation. Folk concepts of time and change, summarized in proposition number 4, are the subject of Chapter 8. And finally, Chapter 9 elaborates on proposition number 5 and the particular type of fatalism it indicates.

5

The Concepts of *Aire* and *Susto*: Symbolic Representations of Perceived Social and Geographic Environment

THE CONCEPTS of *aire* (air or "bad air") and *susto* (fright) are widespread Spanish–American explanations for disease. Aire is mentioned in almost all native descriptions of illness and some forms of it must certainly be New World in origin, while other contemporary aspects stem from the Hippocratic system of hot and cold introduced during the Conquest (Foster 1953:209).[1] The syndrome of susto is an almost equally significant Spanish–American folk concept of disease (*cf.* Gillin 1948:398–399, and Rubel 1964:270–271). Both concepts are among the most enduring Spanish–American alternatives to explanations of sickness and health provided by modern Western medicine. This chapter attempts to explain their persistence by analyzing their meaning in Ixtepeji world view.

Aire

Proposition number 1 (Chapter 4) depicts a negative and anxiety-ridden view of life. It describes a world permeated with mysterious dangers which constantly threaten the individual, a world in which one is never able to attain lasting security. If this proposition correctly describes such a perception of reality, we would expect it to be expressed in folk beliefs. In other words, if the people of Ixtepeji really live in such a mental world there should be some conscious attempt to explain and deal with it, that is, an elaboration of folk beliefs and practices that reflect the underlying assumptions.

Such a symbolic representation that corresponds with, and expresses, the cognitive and affective aspects of the proposition does in fact exist. The element in their environment that symbolizes Ixtepejanos' view of reality is air. By "air" I mean the invisible gases of the atmosphere.

---

[1] Re the variety and area distribution of *aire* beliefs in Mesoamerica. *cf.* Adams and Rubel (1967:338–340).

Why should air be given such a heavy symbolic loading? Let us examine the physical and psychological properties of air and the atmosphere, in order to see how it is in many ways an ideal element to select from the natural world to objectify the subjectivity of the proposition.

First of all, the proposition states that the geographic and social world is filled with ubiquitous, unknown and unknowable dangerous beings and entities, which constantly threaten the individual. Let us consider these attributes individually:

1. *Ubiquity.* Danger is an omnipresent quality of the physical and supernatural world and of social relations. What more suitable thing could serve to symbolize this pervasiveness than the very atmosphere that surrounds and fills the total environment and penetrates into every nook and cranny of it? The nature of air is such that it is not just one of many elements in the natural world among which the individual moves; rather, it is virtually synonymous with the space in which the external world is set, and it is through this atmosphere that one moves. It is unavoidable; *one cannot escape it.* It *presses* in against the body, just at it diffuses in and out of the houses. It is an unavoidable circumstance of life to such an extent that every breath brings the individual into the most intimate and enduring association with it that is imaginable.

2. *Unknown and unknowable.* On a par with the ubiquity of air is the quality of invisibility. Air is everywhere, but it is never seen; one cannot tangibly grasp and comprehend it. Its ultimate nature must remain a mystery to man equipped with only his five naked senses.

3. *Dangerous.* This is not so much an objective quality of air as one ascribed to it by folk belief, as discussed below. Here we may note that Ixtepejanos consider air to be the main natural and supernatural cause of death and disease, which are two of their most serious concerns.

In discussing the Mexican personality, the poet Octavio Paz finds it fitting to use air in an image which fits Ixtepeji.

The harshness and hostility of the environment—and this hidden, indefinable menace that always floats in the air—forces us to close ourselves to the exterior, as these plants of the plateau which accumulate their juices behind a spiny skin (Paz 1959:27; my translation).

Compare Paz's image with the following not atypical dream reported by a middle-aged woman in Ixtepeji.

I was in a deep canyon where I went to fetch some water, when the canyon broke open and water and a tremendous *aigre* (colloquial for *aire*) came roaring out. I thought that the water would stop the aigre, but it couldn't. The aigre was so strong it was stopping my breath, and the water was rising also. There was no place to hide from this aigre. It came from one side and the other. I grabbed my baby and said to it, "We're going to die together," and then sat down under a tree. I turned my face one way and another but this aigre kept hitting me and I couldn't breathe either on one side or the other. This aigre wanted to kill us and I couldn't endure it. I said to the baby, "There is no way to escape; there is nothing but aigre; we are going to die by the aigre." Then I woke up very frightened.

Foster, in speaking about the extent of the aire concept, notes that "its exact nature has an elusive quality which makes discussion difficult" (Foster 1953: 209). Historically, aire is an old, widely diffused Spanish–American concept, but it is apparent that it assumes an extreme form and significance in Ixtepeji. I suggest that the unusual elaboration of the Ixtepeji variety of the aire theme provides a key to the "exact nature" and "elusive quality" that Foster mentions.

We can infer that the air concept is indeed significant from its historic persistence and widespread occurrence. The question is simply, "What function or functions is it fulfilling which account for its significance?" As a tentative answer, I propose that it symbolizes covert aspects of world views that are similar to the one in Ixtepeji. Furthermore, it is precisely the extreme nature of the Ixtepeji world view which give special prominence to the aire theme in Ixtepeji that is lacking elsewhere. I suggest that the aire theme fulfills the same function elsewhere in Spanish–American, but that other less elaborated forms of it correlate with world views that perceive the world as less threatening, dangerous, and awesome than in Ixtepeji, or perhaps where some other belief serves the same function. In regard to this latter possibility, Currier (1966) has argued for a similar symbolic function for the hot–cold system of food classification in Michoacán. But in Ixtepeji there is little concern with food classification. And in the Valley of Oaxaca, where the aire system is also strongly developed, Hendry reports that the hot–cold system is so diminished that there are no references made to hot foods (Hendry 1957: 103).

DETAILS OF THE AIRE SYSTEM   It would be difficult to overemphasize the significance of air in the daily life of Ixtepejanos. The Spanish term "aire" is occasionally uttered, but far more frequent is the colloquialism "aigre" which, in view of its predominant usage by Ixtepejanos, is the form I shall employ. In theory, a distinction can be made between the use of "aigre" to refer to the purely physical nature of the atmosphere, as in the sentence "the air is blowing the leaves," and use of the term to refer to the malevolent qualities of air. In actual practice, however, there is no sharp distinction; all utterances of the term connote in some degree the negative qualities.

Referents of the term range from things that are slightly annoying, anxiety arousing, or mysterious, to situations in which aigre has implications for life and death. For example, in response to the question, "Why is the house full of smoke?" one may answer, "Because there is aigre," or "Because the wind outside won't let the smoke escape through the roof." Such an utterance is seemingly about a simple natural phenomenon, but it is affectively tinged by the insidious nature of aigre, which is causing discomfort for mysterious and unknowable reasons. In another instance the explanation for the sudden death of a supposedly healthy individual might be simply, "He died of aigre."

There is a slight tendency toward the usage of "aire" instead of "aigre" in utterances where the referent has relatively nonmalevolent and nonmysterious qualities. A man from Ixtepeji went to Oaxaca City one day where he saw military paratroopers jump near the edge of town. Back in Ixtepeji he animatedly described the action of the parachutes, how they impeded the jumper's fall through the "aire." But upon questioning by others as to how such an extraordinary thing was possible he, uncertain of the mystery himself, reverted to the use of "aigre." The term is so laden with symbolic meanings and associations that it is difficult to isolate any completely neutral usages of it. Folk beliefs state that air is intrinsically mysterious and dangerous.

"Aigre" is, in effect, a generic term that subsumes, in a folk classification, three distinct types.[2] This folk taxonomy of aigres is another indication of the negative qualities of aigre, and, by virtue of taxomic elaboration, of its significance in the belief system. Aigres are classified as follows:

1. *Aigre natural* (natural air): This type has the least consequence for the well-being of humans. It results mainly from simple chilling in accordance with the Hippocratian concepts of hot and cold mixing. Sickness resulting from this aigre is referred to as being sent by God (*enfermedades de Dios*), and is usually treated with household remedies such as herbs or patent medicines. Treatment is therefore relatively inexpensive. The most frequent symptom of *aigre natural* is a sharp ache in the nape of the neck.[3]

2. *Aigre puesto* (placed air): This air is literally placed or sent into the body of a victim by an enemy. The most common method is the sympathetic magic practice of fabricating an effigy doll of the victim and then sticking pins or mud in the stomach or head. This causes a bad aigre to enter the same part of the victim causing him pain and possibly killing him. In contrast to *aigre natural*, this is more serious and requires expensive treatment by a special curer.

3. *Aigre de hora*: This term is not easily translated; literally it means "air of the hour." It too is a type of *aigre puesto*, but the agent and method of infliction are different. Whereas *aigre puesto* is inflicted by humans using techniques of black magic, *aigre de hora* is a specialty of various supernatural beings who are dangerous at night and during certain hours of special days of the year. The beings who inflict most *aigre de hora* are known as *brujos de lumbre*, or "fire witches." They are called fire witches because it is their custom to fly through the sky as balls of fire, a phenomenon people of the town occasionally report. There is some confusion as to the exact status of the fire witches. According to some informants, they are spiritual counterparts of actual living people in the town who have the power to transform themselves to this other state of being. Others describe them as a special type of spirit of the dead, a lost soul. Regardless of their exact nature, there is agreement that they are an organized group with a leader and hierarchy that roughly parallels the civil hierarchy of the town. Collectively, they are spoken of as "the vigilance," which refers to the belief that at night, when the civil authority is not functioning, except for the young men of the *policía,* the fire witches go on duty to *vigilar el pueblo*, which means to protect the town from outside danger and to maintain peace within.

The fire witches each evening assemble where they receive instructions from their chief, who then dispatches them to their posts for the night. It is going to and from these meetings that they are observed flying through the sky, or as is said in Ixtepeji *por el aigre* (through the air). Some of them are assigned duty in different parts of town; others are sent to crosses on hills, which form a protective ring around the town. The main purpose of this second mission is to prevent evil winds and diseases from blowing into Ixtepeji from neighboring towns.

---

[2] For a similar tripartite taxonomy of *aires* among the Chorti of Guatemala, *cf.* Wisdom (1940:317–319).

[3] The same ailment is also common among Mexican–Americans in the United States and usually is diagnosed by physicians as "tension headache" due to anxiety (Clyde Woods, M.D., personal communication).

Wood crosses on the edge of the town.

Although one of the presumed functions of the fire witches is protection from foreign dangers threatening the town, they also act upon townspeople themselves for various reasons, but mainly for going about at night on illicit business, which includes everything from actual criminal activity such as stealing and witchcraft to mild carousing or going on errands. In effect, there is a curfew each night enforced by "the vigilance." The main way they punish violators is by placing a bad aigre in them. This curfew is enforced more stringently during certain hours of the night than others, hence the term *aigre de hora*.

AIRE-RELATED CONCEPTS Air is the predominant symbol representing the mysterious and nefarious aspects of the environment. But, along with air, there are several other air-like and air-related folk beliefs that serve the same function; one is the belief in various types of spirits.

Spirits. Spirits of the dead have various social roles in Ixtepeji, but viewed in another way they are an analogue of the aigre theme. Just as the world is permeated with air, so is it permeated with spirits—spirits which, like the air, are invisible, mysterious, unpredictable, threatening, and as close to one as the air he breathes. This psychological tendency to associate spirits with air and breathing is by no means unique to Ixtepejanos. In the Bible, for example, we find Satan referred to as "the prince of the power of the air, the spirit that now worketh in the children of disobedience" (Eph.2:2). Frazer was perhaps the first anthropologist to point out the widespread identification of breath and spirit. This identity is also revealed in the common linguistic association of the two in one word. For example, in Latin *spiritus* mean both "breath" and "spirit," and from it have been derived such English words as *aspire, inspire, expire,* and *conspire,* all of which suggest the idea of spirit-breath going into or out of the body.

In Spanish *espíritu* (spirit) has, like its English cognate, lost the denotation of "breath," but the breath-like, air-like nature of an *espíritu* is in no way diminished. And again, in addition to the neutral qualities that Ixtepeji spirits share with aigre, such as invisibility, they have the same complement of negative psychological traits, malevolence, and uncontrollability. In addition to the intrinsic aigre-like nature of spirits, their identification with aigre is underscored by the method of attack whereby they, as other malevolent beings, place bad aigre in a victim.

In Ixtepeji, concern with and anxiety about spirits, especially the spirits of dead relatives, reaches a climax during the fiesta of *Todos Santos,* or All Souls Day. The importance of this celebration is attested to by the fact that Ixtepejanos expend more resources on it than on any other fiesta, for during this period the spirits return to visit their families and to feast with them. Of course, since they are spirits they do not eat the special morsels prepared for them, but they do partake of the aromas and vapors that the food gives off into the air.

The negative qualities of spirits and aigre also in part explain the common use of *copal,* an incense made from pine pitch. Copal is burned in quantity at all religious events in the church, homes, street processions, and elsewhere. It is also burned on house altars at different times, especially at fiestas, and it is used in some curing practices. To the question "Why is copal burned around cadavers?" a woman replied, "Because the Devil wants to be with the body, but the copal scares him. It also keeps him out of the house. If someone is afraid of him, they burn copal. It is also burned at masses to make the Devil run. Also it scares lost spirits, lost souls, and aigres." A man said about the use of copal in curing, "It's a strong remedy against bad aigres; the smoke removes the disease one carries just as a lighted cigarette carried when you are out at night guards against lost aigres which blow through the streets. They hit us and we don't know what hit us." This last sentence well expresses the insidious, unpredictable quality of aigre. If cigarettes are not at hand, a burning ember or censer will protect someone who must go on an errand that cannot await the light of day. The preference for copal to ward off aigre and aigre-like entities seems to lie in the large billows of pungent smoke it produces. Smoke is an aigre-like phenomenon, but one that men can control; whereas aigre is invisible, smoke is visible, real and not illusory, and it is sanctified by the Church.

Naguales. As is common throughout Mesoamerica, there is a belief in Ixtepeji that certain people have the power to transform themselves into animals (Foster 1944; Holland 1961; Villa Rojas 1963; Vogt 1965). These animals are called *naguales* or *animales naguales.* The most common in Ixtepeji are coyotes, snakes, bats, and foxes. Cougars and jaguars may also be naguales.

There are several main themes associated with the nagual belief. People with this power transform themselves into animals only to harm others. As with witchcraft, the prime motivation is envy, and the most common method of attack is to kill the victim's animals, thus causing him expense. Also, naguales are very cunning and deceptive. For example, *coyote nagual* can open a cleverly closed chicken house and make watchdogs go to sleep.

Analyzed in terms of the aigre theme, naguales show certain aigre-like qualities. They are malevolent and dangerous and, as in the case of aigre, the forms in which they manifest themselves are common features in the natural landscape, things against which it is virtually impossible to protect oneself because they are able to penetrate even the best defensive measures.

Woman sitting in doorway of her kitchen.

The following is a rather typical nagual incident:

> Pablo killed a female coyote near his chickens, skinned it, and threw it in the fire. The next day a stranger came and said he had heard about the coyote and asked for a piece of it. Pablo wondered: "Was it her husband? How did he know where to come?" Pablo told the stranger that he knew nothing about the coyote but the man insisted that it was killed there and that he be given a piece of it. Pablo finally grabbed his gun and chased the man away. Pablo surmised that since the man was unable to retrieve a piece of the dead coyote, he was unable to revive his wife who would thus stay dead. He concluded by saying, "One doesn't know how and when they go about or where they are."

This incident and the telling of it reveal the same basic fears and anxieties associated with aigre. The last sentence clearly expresses the aigre-like qualities of naguales.

"Ugly Animals." The aigre-like symbolic and emotional significance of *animales naguales* is an elaboration of ideas and emotions associated with the natural animal world. Like aigre, domestic and wild animals are found everywhere in the environment. In the fields and woods around town live the larger wild species such as coyotes, deer, and the occasional cougar. The town itself is virtually crawling with the smaller forms of animal life. The many stone walls around house plots and the gardens and the adobe house walls and tile roofs are ideal habitats for numerous species of lizards and snakes. Rats and mice are abundant also, especially at night when the reptiles are quiet. They make their own distinctive sounds running along the rafters, gnawing on cartons, or dragging ears of corn. It is not uncommon for them to run across the blanket or face of a sleeping person. The simple construction of houses allows complete freedom of passage in and out to all small creatures. The mild tropical climate is conducive to insects and spiders, which exist in profusion. And, in the air over the town on any day of the year are the ever-circling *zopilotes*, or vultures, so graceful in the air and grotesque on the ground.

Ixtepejanos' beliefs concerning wild animals are, in certain respects, irrational and based more on emotional premises than on acual fact. For example, in folk tales, even the benign deer appears as a menacing creature. Also, many varieties of snakes are common, most of which are small rodent predators, quite harmless to humans. Poisonous snakes, including rattlesnakes, are rare. But to questions such as, "Are there poisonous snakes here," the usual reply is, "All snakes are poisonous." Dr. Herbert Eder has informed me that in coastal Oaxaca as well, all snakes are considered deadly poisonous and objects of great fear, and De La Fuente (1949:318) notes that *susto de culebra* (*cf.* below) is the strongest kind of fright in nearby Yalalag.

Some snakes are ascribed attributes that are now familiar aigre qualities. *La lechera* (milkmaid) is so called because, when killed, milk flows from its wounds. It has the power to make people fall asleep, especially a mother. It then sucks at her breast while sticking its tail in her child's mouth so it will not cry. *La flecha* (the arrow) is very thin and light and is said to fly *through the air.* "It bites us if it can seize us. Sometimes it frightens us when it passes by rapidly. It bites one if they do not see it."

Ordinarily whenever men see snakes they attempt to kill them. If other people are present, they rapidly circle around, with men and boys throwing rocks at the helpless victim and beating it with sticks, while women and girls stand in the background drawing their shawls in front of their faces. Lizards evoke similar, but much less intense reactions. The very common occurrence of lizards—they are constantly running up and down the walls of houses, inside and out, across the ground and over the rocks—precludes such a response every time one is seen. Most Ixtepejanos, however, falsely think several types are poisonous.

The snake is the animal that most dramatically symbolizes aigre qualities. Its natural form lends itself to this function; it is silent and, because of protective coloring and shape, very difficult to perceive and thus it has deceptive or invisible qualities. Add to this its ability, suddenly and without warning, to inject deadly poison into an unsuspecting victim, and we have a cluster of traits that compose one more replication of the aigre theme.

Injuries inflicted by animals are treated by home remedies, usually some medicinal plant. It is significant, however, that in the case of snake bite, what might be called an extreme remedy is indicated. It is a mixture of cacao and human feces, which, to be effective, must be drunk immediately after the bite.

In answering questions about the significance of a rattlesnake's buzzing, no informant expressed the thought that it was a warning signal. The implication I draw from this is that, in accordance with the aigre theme, one does not conceive dangerous entities in the world as giving warnings. On the contrary, they actively attempt to deceive and trick the unwary victim and then to strike when he is off guard.

One of the most common dream themes, for both men and women, is that they are being chased by "ugly animals" who are threatening to catch and bite them. And in another variant of this dream, hideous animals eat the flesh of the dreamer who is paralyzed and unable to protect himself. Also, according to folk beliefs, dreams in which "ugly animals" appear always forbode a calamitous event, either for the dreamer or his family. Dreams of being paralyzed by aigre are also common. In this type of dream an aigre presses on the dreamer's chest such that he cannot breathe and suffocates.

Mal Ojo. Several other Spanish–American folk beliefs and practices can be interpreted in light of the *aire* concept. A final example is *mal ojo* (evil-eye sickness), a condition to which children often succumb as a result of a glance by someone possessing "strong vision." ". . . the evil eye is, to some extent, a reflection of envy. This force enters people or things not belonging to the viewer who desires or envies them" (Madsen 1964:75–76). The evil eye is, like aigre, as difficult to avoid as the glance of a neighbor, and it too enters the body to harm it.

Susto, Spirits, and Death

The common Spanish–American belief in *susto,* or *espanto,* is a significant aspect of Ixtepeji folk belief. Susto, the preferred term in Ixtepeji, is caused by any sudden, frightening encounter with humans, animals, inanimate objects, or supernatural beings. Two consequences may result from a susto: the soul, or spirit, of the person may leave the body, or the body may become susceptible to an attack of bad air which will enter the weakened body.

Children are thought to be especially prone to susto, the most common cause being a fall or some other abrupt physical trauma. After the child has stopped its initial crying it may become very *triste*, or lethargic, and sleep a great deal; in extreme cases it may become autistic, or as is said, act like a *somnámbulo* or "sleep-walker." One treatment for susto in children is intentionally to give the affected child another susto which cures the first in accord with the saying, "One susto removes another."

While susto is primarily an affliction of children, it is by no means limited to them and is second only to aigre in the etiology of adult ailments, especially in women. The two notions are often combined as mentioned above, but are conceptually distinct insofar as treatment for them is different; in the case of an attack of aigre precipitated by a susto, both the aigre and the susto may be treated.

A woman of Ixtepeji who has been crippled for about ten years with what appears to be an advanced case of rheumatoid arthritis, illustrates how susto may affect an adult. One day a man was being chased by some others; he entered her house to hide while she was away on an errand. The other men found him there and killed him. Someone went to notify her, which along with the sight of the dead man gave her the susto. Another case: Four years ago Lucía Medina, then a strong woman of twenty-two, received a terrible susto from which she is still suffering. She had just left her cousin's house with her cousin, a woman of the same age. The street was very dark. All of a sudden her cousin's husband, who had just returned to town, came running after them threatening his wife with a pistol. Lucía ran home crying violently and subsequently became extremely lethargic for one year. She spent almost all of this time in bed, having only enough strength to go out into the sun occasionally to warm herself. She stopped eating almost completely, and became "as thin as a skeleton," and is just now starting to fill out the clothes she wore before the susto. During this period she slept almost continually, waking only to eat. She suffered from a great *tristeza*, or depression, and one month later sharp pains began in her head, neck, arms, and legs. She frequently burst into spontaneous crying spells when she thought about the man coming after her—*como la muerte* (like death). As she says, "I could think of no other thing." Local curers explained her ailment as due to a "strong air" that had entered her body since the susto was at night.

Closely related to the concept of susto is the belief of *mala muerte*, or "bad death." The manner of death is crucial to the well-being and relative contentment of the spirit. A mala muerte results from any event that kills the individual suddenly without warning, such as an accident or a murder. Such a death is very distinct from a *buena muerte*, or "good death," which occurs inevitably from sickness, the only natural cause of death, or when the person dies in his own house, is immediately dressed in clean clothes, and candles are lit. In order to have a buena muerte, it is also important that the person was not only comfortable in his own house but that his relatives were taking care of him and giving him good food to eat. For an individual to experience a buena muerte is of concern not only to himself, but also to his relatives, who would otherwise be the subjects of his spirit's unhappiness for having suffered a mala muerte. Accounts of malas muertes are common and in most cases the living relatives attempt to appease the discontented spirit, who usually signals his presence and displeasure by making buzzing sounds in the house at night, turning over objects, and so forth.

An inevitable correlate of a mala muerte is a grand susto. "Bad death" is in effect the prototype of all sustos. All lesser sustos are in this sense minor replications of what happens in the case of a mala muerte.

Since beliefs and practices pertaining both to the susto and mala muerte concepts are conceptually and empirically related, we may talk of a *susto-mala muerte* belief complex. Given this nexus of ideas and practices, we may ask what function it fulfills and what maintains it in the folk belief system. Could it, like the aire system, be symbolizing certain aspects of the perceived social and geographic environment? In this regard, the following description of the experiential qualities of the Mexican environment, which is certainly true of Ixtepeji, is in accord with the *susto-mala muerte* pattern:

> Psychologically the Mexican milieu is underlaid with an ingrained morbidity that derives from the traumatic character of Mexican experience. All of life— personal, social, political, and even cultural—is burdened by the *expectancy of sudden injury, violence, and death.* The very physical environment seems to fit in with this description of the universe. The sudden earthquake, the unexpected, newly-born volcano, the rapid change of weather that in an hour turns a balmy warmth to shivering cold accompanied by a flood of water pouring down from the sky, or that brings the hard-winddriven hail that flattens the crops, are common experiences. Equally certain is the sudden disease—even if only smallpox or typhoid. . . . Above all there is the possible appearance of armed men who rob and kill and destroy. There is a kind of *expectancy of death—sudden and meaningless*—that makes fatalism and indifference to life a common feature of all groups and of all classes (Tannenbaum 1950:16–17; italics mine).

With the exception of a volcanic eruption, the above calamities are all experiences that have shaped and are still shaping the attitudes Ixtepejanos have about the conditions of their lives.

The hypothesis that the concepts of susto and mala muerte serve a symbolic function is reinforced by events in early childhood which can be seen as instilling these attitudes, especially susto.

Ixtepeji is a society in which there is much suppressed hostility, or *muina* (*cf.* Chapter 7). This suppression is largely a defense mechanism. Since a person who displays muina is defined as a potential threat to others (e.g. prone to perform witchcraft), those who perceive the muina in him are apt to take counter measures. To avoid these counter measures one therefore tries to avoid displaying negative emotions. Such emotions will, however, find some relatively safe form of expression and object to be vented on.[4] The privacy of one's home affords one such situa-

---

[4] Whiting and Child (1953:273–276) demonstrate cross-cultural correlations that support the hypothesis that societies whose members have strong anxiety about aggression trained into them in the course of socialization tend to attribute aggression to other people or to spirits, rather than admit it to themselves. "The general perception of the social and supernatural world developed in such a society should be one of a world in which a number of potentially very aggressive agents reside" (1953:275). In other words, such a society should have a projective system comparable to the *aire* system.

tion, and animals and children afford safe objects. Parents usually tolerate the common annoyances of children with patience, but at times their limits are overstrained. Then a mother may suddenly punctuate her low murmuring talk to her child with a string of harsh abuses, a slap on the head, or a well aimed stick of firewood. These sudden alternations from gentleness to harshness, and from acceptance to rejection, plus a prevalent practice of controlling children by lies and threats, are daily experiences in the childhood of most villages, which cannot but instill a sense of insecurity and an inability to predict when warmth and security may suddenly disappear.[5] These ways of relating to children are exacerbated in many parents under the influence of alcohol. Alcoholism is endemic in Ixtepeji, and alcohol lowers the ability to suppress muina. Children are ill equipped to predict when a benevolent father, who leaves them with a kiss in the morning, will return at night, transformed by alcohol into an overbearing patriarch. It is while men are drunk that most child- and wife-beatings occur. Again, the important point here is the abruptness with which children experience these transformations that their parents undergo, and their inability to predict them. Furthermore, there is the above mentioned practice of treating childhood susto by giving the child another, intentional susto.

The manner in which children are weaned also fits this pattern. The age of weaning is variable, but usually coincides with the onset of the mother's next pregnancy. What is uniform, however, is the *suddenness* with which it is done. Similar observations are reported by the Romneys from the Mixtec town of Juxtlahuaca, Oaxaca.

> The most striking uniformity of weaning is the abruptness with which it takes place. . . . Half of the mothers used a bitter herb or dirt on the breast to discourage nursing. . . . Just over a third of the mothers reported that they used the technique of leaving the child with a relative for a couple of days. Thus we see that although there is variation in the time of weaning and in the techniques used, there is almost complete uniformity in the abruptness with which weaning takes place (Romney and Romney 1966:103–104).

Currier also gives evidence that weaning is sudden and traumatic in Michoacán, and says it is, "difficult to see how most children could fail to make an intense and indelible association between the unanticipated and concurrent experience of rejection and deprivation of physical warmth. It is to be expected that such an association be carried into adult life by almost every member of Mexican peasant society . . ." (Currier 1966:259–260).

One further aspect of susto should be mentioned. De la Fuente notes that in Yalalag souls that are lost from susto remain in the ground or in water (1949:318). It is significant that in Ixtepeji souls lost from susto and mala muerte remain in the air. The air is becoming continually more populated with malevolent spirits, an indication, in accord with Proposition number 4, that the total environment is changing for the worse.

---

[5] Whiting and Child (1953:265–269) also give cross-cultural evidence that supports the hypothesis that fear of other people and of spirits arises by generalization from fear of parents acquired through severe socialization practices. The Ixtepeji data support this hypothesis, viz., that high socialization anxiety, caused by parental behavior that teaches the child to fear frustration and active punishment, generalizes to a fear of *aire* and other *aire*-like phenomena.

These data on susto support an epidemiological model advanced by Rubel (1964), who argues that the susto syndrome develops in response to various stressful social situations, in which the salient feature is "role helplessness" (*cf.* also O'Nell and Selby 1968). In a cross-cultural perspective there are other culturally determined responses to social stress. This present examination has therefore sought to explain the presence of the susto concept in Ixtepeji culture by relating its symbolic functions to other aspects of Ixtepeji experience and world view.

Summary

Anthropological literature on the folk concepts of aire and susto have considered them separately, and dealt mainly with areal distribution, symptomatology, treatment, and epidemiology. This chapter has sought to demonstrate (1) how both concepts are psychologically interrelated, and (2) that aire, susto, and related folk beliefs serve as symbols reflecting perception of the social and geographic environments of Ixtepeji; they symbolize the ubiquity of perceived hostile forces and the unpredictable suddenness with which they attack.

6

Appearances Cannot Be Trusted

P ROPOSITION NUMBER 2 (Chapter 4) stated that, "Human and supernatural aggression are performed through deceit and deception." Because of this covert belief, man sees himself as constantly on the defensive against this form of aggression. The way in which this belief affects man's relations to other men and to the local environment is the subject of this chapter.

The Concept of *Engaño*

One of the most prevalent concepts in Ixtepeji world view is the assumption of the widespread existence of *engaño*, or deception and trickery. As Ixtepejanos commonly use the verb *engañar* it means, "to deceive by lying or otherwise altering appearances so that an unwary victim will let his defenses down, allowing the person or thing performing the engaño to take advantage of him." Supernatural entities most commonly perform engaño by transforming themselves into something that the victim is not apt to suspect. Supernatural engaño is discussed elsewhere (Chapter 11), but it is to be noted that the principles and associated attitudes are the same in other areas of life.

Because belief in engaño colors so much perception of social reality, it generates a second related attitude of basic distrust, expressed by the term *desconfianza*. Desconfianza and engaño are thought to be widespread; as a proverb says, "Here we are all sinners." Desconfianza in others is logically related to and reinforces individualism. Because the individual assumes engaño to be a basic potential motivation in others, he distrusts them and thus turns to his own personal resources as the main way of defending himself.

One of the most insidious aspects of engaño and desconfianza is the way in which they are self perpetuating when looked at in terms of reciprocal social interaction. As pointed out above, the assumption that engaño is basic in human relations moves the individual to protect himself against it. Secondly, the individual believes he is most open to engaño when his adversary is aware of his personal situation. To protect himself from them one must therefore conceal his actual state of affairs so that it will not become public knowledge and so used to his disadvantage. The logic of the situation is such that this is best done by creating other impressions of what one's real situation is. In other words, one must create counter deceptions that will mislead potential antagonists. The end result of such behavior is to maintain a high level of intentional deception, which is a form of self-fulfilling prophecy. This is well expressed in the often stated proverb, *El amigo más amigo es el más traidor,* "the best friend is the worst traitor." Similar in its logic to this proverb is the custom, when offering a drink to someone from a personal bottle, of taking the first swallow, "to prove that it isn't poison."

The theme of engaño is common in folk tales and jokes that center on an ironic double-cross. This is demonstrated in the following variation on the fable of "Androcles and the Lion," which was told by a man who knew it only as "a very funny story." When Androcles is thrown into the arena with the lions, the one that he had helped earlier recognizes him and tells the other lions not to harm him—because, since he already knows him, he is going to eat him himself!

The following additional examples show how these concepts operate. On several occasions when I went to Oaxaca City, the Avendaño family gave me letters to mail there. They could easily have posted the letters in the town and thus have had them carried to Ixtlán; this would have taken longer, but time was not a factor in their thinking. What worried them was that someone would open the letter and read it. They described in detail the route the letter would take to Mexico and approximately how many hands it would pass through in Ixtepeji, Ixtlán, Oaxaca, and Mexico. None of them feared that the letter would not arrive, only that it would be opened and read. Also, they expressed no concern that it be opened in Oaxaca or Mexico, but only in the *municipio* or in Ixtlán, which were precisely the two places that would be by-passed if it were mailed in Oaxaca. In other words, they were concerned that someone in town or in Ixtlán, would read the letter and learn of their affairs, something that would be inconsequential should it happen as far away as Oaxaca or Mexico. Another instance is similar. Doña Nicolasa, who is illiterate, occasionally asked me to write letters for her, although there were many other persons who could have done this favor for her. She also asked me to read all of her mail to her, although this sometimes meant waiting several days. A large part of this correspondence was with relatives in Mexico, discussing attempts to sell her house. Presumably the main reason that she asked me to do this was that I would not be staying in town permanently and as such would be a safer risk than other acquaintances. She once expressed this in a letter apologizing for a tardy reply to a niece in Mexico by explaining that she had to wait for my return to write the letter because, "it gives me much pain that the people here should know what I tell you."

Although stealing and housebreaking are rare, there is much concern about them, and seemingly unnecessary precautions are taken. I was repeatedly warned by friends that I should never leave valuables in my house or leave it unattended. This generalized distrust of fellow townspeople extends in varying degrees to one's neighbors and is cause for much worry over possessions such as turkeys, chickens, and other animals, which must forage about town. Doña Nicolasa often told how, at times when she forgot about her turkeys, they wandered out on the street and were chased down the hill by bad children, adding that there are many bad people around who cannot be trusted.

Family relation is not considered to be a guarantee against engaño, and it is assumed that in all economic dealings with relatives of other households the rules of the marketplace will prevail. It is also undesirable for relatives of other households to have any unnecessary knowledge of one's affairs. The following incident is typical. One afternoon I was walking down the street past the house of Hermelinda Martínez. She asked me if I could come in and look at a bad skin ailment on her sister-in-law's arms to see if something could be done for it. As I was leaving she became very insistent about knowing where I was going. I evasively said, "over there to talk to some people." She persisted and finally asked me exactly who they were, and I said Sebastian Acevedo and his family. She then assumed a very confidential manner and asked me not to mention to them that I was going to help her sister-in-law, even though they are her (Hermelinda's) relatives. I asked her why and she repeated a number of times that it would just be better if they did not know. The compulsion to conceal one's affairs is so strong that Ixtepejanos habitually are reluctant to reveal even the most insignificant personal information. For example, when one town citizen meets another on the street and asks him where he is going, the inevitable reply is *paseando* or *mandado*, that is, "just going for a walk," or "going on an errand."

A person with a reputation for blatantly performing engaños is referred to by the derogatory epithet, *chiripero*. One of the main characteristics of a chiripero is that he will convince the person he plans to deceive that he is well qualified to perform some service, for which the victim will pay him. Rufina Peña is said to be such a person, and although this is the insidious explanation for how she makes much of her money, it is not without foundation. Older women tell how she serves as midwife, although she has no real knowledge, and uses crude techniques, but in spite of this she is able to command fees of up to 100 pesos, whereas the usual charge is only 40 or 50. Her critics are ready to point out that two of her patients died recently under her hands.

Just as engaño is thought to be an aspect of the immediate social relationships within the town, so is it considered a characteristic of the outer world. This is evidenced by the mixed emotions and precautions with which people leave the town either for short trips or for extended lengths of time, and by many other ways in which they express attitudes about the outer world. Since to most townspeople the greater world is perplexing and largely unknown, "the government" serves as a symbol to represent it. While there is a strong scapegoat element in this negative attitude toward "the government," the manner in which these attitudes are expressed reveals that it is seen as an exploitative entity that uses its special powers to further the ends of those in it, to the detriment of the townspeople. The government, state and federal, levies "unfair taxes" on traders "which must be avoided if one is to survive," and imposes many other nuisances such as confiscating the firearms of people walking on the highway. Victims of this practice assert that the police later resell the arms for their personal gain. The government is held responsible for the economic stagnation of the Sierra because it will not invest the capital necessary to get the mines back into operation, but as one informant said, "If they did they would sell all the gold and silver to foreigners, as they do at the mines in Natividad, and not allow any of the local people to profit." There is a joke that the reason there are so many rats present is because the government rounded up rats in Mexico City and dropped them in the mountains. The town was given a choice whether they wanted rats or snakes, so they naturally took the rats.

Just as the outer world is viewed as dangerous, so representatives from it are viewed with special suspicion. In general, until proven otherwise, all outsiders coming into town are assumed to be there with ulterior motives. In 1966 several Baha'i missionaries came on four different occasions to distribute religious pamphlets and interest townspeople in their religion. The townspeople greeted the missionaries with a reserved hospitality and promises to read the literature. But after the missionaries left, people asked in effect what their gimmick was. My explaining that I thought they had no ulterior motives was met with strong doubt and such phrases as, "They think they can trick us (*engañarnos*), but they can't." In all speculations and derision of the Baha'i missionaries, religious factors were almost nonexistent. But they did pose a perplexing problem to Ixtepejanos. Given the underlying assumption that they were there with bad intentions, there was considerable anxiety when such presumed ulterior motives did not become readily apparent. Many individuals responded by assuming that the engaño must therefore have been more insidious than usual.

But in the case of most outsiders, the townspeople consider themselves fairly astute at figuring out what the strangers are up to. There was little doubt that the contractors, hired by the government to design and help the town construct a water system, were out to cheat the town as much as possible on materials and quality.

Childhood Insecurity and *Engaño*

Parents believe it necessary to start disciplining children well before the age of cognizance of right and wrong behavior, to insure instilling proper habits in them. They are quick to assert that children who are not disciplined when young will not obey when they are older. Worse, they will be disrespectful and neglectful of their parents and will not, as adults, fulfill their proper family and community obligations. The parental conception of child training is essentially a Pavlovian model, with emphasis on negative rather than positive conditioning. Aurelia Guzmán summed this up one day after interceding in a quarrel among her children: "When they are fighting, I find out which one is guilty and spank him; that settles it. If you don't say anything to them, they won't be afraid of you. You must scold them and make them mind when they are small, then when they are older and you scold them, they won't get mad."

These ideas are intentionally instilled in children by telling quasi parable accounts of good versus bad daughters and sons. Such speech events are usually dramatically told while the children listen in silence with lowered heads.

The preferred method of disciplining children is to cause them *vergüenza,* or "shame," by laughing at them and making jokes about them. If this fails, they may be frightened by scaring them with some frightening entity or by spanking them.

As to corporal punishment, informants note that some parents are too harsh with their children and beat them with firewood, large wooden spoons, and so forth. Such acts are usually spontaneous explosions of anger and frustration by adults who have come to the end of their patience, rather than planned acts with lectures. Parents recognize that beating children in this fashion is bad, the reason being that it can cause them physical harm, especially to the lungs. Psychological or emotional effects on the children are not a matter of concern. But no parent is apt to refrain from spankings from time to time as a necessary measure for discipline and formation of good character. In this regard there is a saying, "On one side the bread, on the other side the horsewhip," which points up the love a good child will get versus the punishment a bad one will receive. But in actual practice the distinction between positive and negative rewards is not clear cut and depends for the most part on the mood and disposition of the adult. Since people tend to conceal bad moods, especially *muina* (*cf.* Chapter 7), the child is at a disadvantage in predicting adult response to his actions. A parent's affect toward a child often rapidly changes, either from positive to negative or negative to positive. An example: While Aurelia Guzmán was sitting on the floor, little Tomás was annoying her and trying to get at her breast to nurse. She gently pushed him away several times, and then suddenly hit him on the forehead, causing him to burst into tears. He lay down on the floor and cried. Immediately after hitting him she calmly gave him a banana so he would stop crying.

Although informants say causing children vergüenza is the preferred way of keeping them in line, in actual practice the use of deception is far more common. Two types of deception are used. If a parent or some adult wishes a child to do some particular thing or behave in some particular manner, they are apt to tell them that they will grant them some special favor. Adults use these ploys most commonly when things are running smoothly and they wish to change the course of the child's activities. Parents often make such promises with no intention of fulfilling them. A second type of deception is more likely to be used by harried parents trying to cope with cranky children. Here a threat, which the adult has no intention of carrying out, is made to the child so as to frighten him into submission to the parent's will. The most common form of this strategy is to tell the child that if he does not obey he will be given to *La Llorona* (*cf.* Chapter 11), the coyote, the dog, the owl, or any animal of which he has a special fear. The coyote is something of a prototype for any number of threatening, frightening entities that may be used by saying for example, "Here comes the Coyote. Do you want to go with the Coyote? Do you want him to take you?" Parents may also threaten to sell a child to a strange adult who is present.[1]

---

[1] Parsons says that in Mitla, "To stop an older child crying it may be told that the owl . . . will come . . . and carry it away (the owl is the messenger of death) or it may be threatened with the cat . . ." (1936:87).

Occasionally when a harassed parent, usually the mother, is especially frustrated in her efforts to silence a child, she will take him out of the house and tell him she is going to leave him there for some animal to get. A variation of this threatened abandonment occurs while traveling, when parents may stop along some desolate stretch of road and tell a crying child that they are going to leave him there if he does not stop crying.

At times vergüenza and threat of rejection may be used together. In December when nights were cold, Raul bought two new wool blankets in Oaxaca City. At dinner on the evening he returned, his two younger brothers were huddling in them. Their mother took this moment to remark rhetorically that Pastor, the younger one, sometimes urinates in his sleep, and then told him that if he urinated on the new blankets he was going to go outside and sleep with the dog on bean sacks in front of the house.

When little Esperanza has *muina*, she often goes behind her house and throws rocks and dirt clods on the roof of the kitchen where her antagonists are inside. One such occasion was at lunch when her mother scolded her for teasing her little brother. When she came back in sometime later, her mother scolded her again and said to her brother-in-law who was in the kitchen, "Is it true that they are throwing bad children in the jail?" He replied in a matter-of-fact tone that it was true, that he had already thrown four in himself, since he was the municipal secretary. This caused Esperanza to draw close to her mother and pull the folds of her skirt about her. Her father then lent further credibility to this deception by saying he had just seen the children's mothers come to nurse them through the bars.

The engendering of fear in the child is consciously intended in such deceptions. For example: Late one evening Hilaria was in her kitchen with her son, Alonso, who had just taken baby Teodoro into the house from where he had been sleeping on the floor. He soon began to cry and Hilaria told Alonso, who huddled next to the fire, to go to Teodoro and tell him the Cat was coming. Asked about this, she replied that children are often told such things as for example, "Go to sleep because the Cat is coming and he will eat you." She continued, "This is how we scare the babies. Also when a dog barks one says, 'He's going to eat you!' " But such ruses often backfire as the child becomes more frightened, as happened in this instance, and in a few moments Alonso returned to the kitchen with the wailing child. In frustration Hilaria decided to tie him onto her back saying roughly, "Be quiet, I'm carrying you now." While she was tying him on her back, Alonso hit him on the back of the head a few times causing him to cry again. She scolded him and said softly to the baby, "Alonso hit you? Did he? Do you want to hit him back with a stick?" She cooed to him like this for a while, but after she was silent he began to cry again. This evoked from her a harsh, "Shut up! Here comes the Cat." Then in a few moments, she was gently murmuring to him again.

These rapid alternations from rejection to acceptance and from harshness to gentleness, plus the practices of lying to and threatening children relate to the insecurity characteristic of the world view, which sees reality as deceptive, illusory, and menacing. It is important to realize the significance of such experiences in the daily life of children, for it is literally at the mother's breast that the child learns his first lessons in lying and engaño. An example from field notes:

> While eating lunch this afternoon, Hilaria was holding baby Teodoro who was starting to talk. He was cranky and whining and wanted to nurse, and was irritating his mother. Several times she turned her chest away so he could not get at her breast. She said several times, "You want some breast, do you? Well you can't because a rat already came and ate it." After doing this for a while, causing him to verge on crying, she gave him her breast.

Although lying to and frightening children are the prevalent ways of disciplining them, there are occasions for gentleness and tenderness. On rare occasions a mother will softly sing lullabies to a crying child. Mothers themselves recognize the greater efficacy and desirability of gentleness over frightening children. As one put it, "A little song is more effective because singing to them makes them go to sleep, but with *susto* they just close their mouths and no more."

From the above discussion and examples, we can draw several generalizations about the methods parents use to discipline children and make them conform to adult wishes. These practices bear obvious correspondence to the world view. Most significant is the use of deception and fear, and real or threatened rejection or abandonment. Second is the inconsistent—from the child's point of view, unpredictable—use of positive and negative reward. Parents are, like God, capricious and all powerful.

Ilusión

An adjective that Ixtepejanos often use is *legítimo* (legitimate), which expresses the idea that something is genuine, real, and can be trusted. For example, a tool may be made of "legitimate" steel, the "real thing," as opposed to some inferior metal. Or clothing may be said to be "legitimate" wool, or a particular brand, rather than an imitation. In the market place and in commercial transactions in general, there is much concern to protect oneself from fraud. (Analysis of law cases, in 1964, in the neighboring district of Villa Alta, revealed that complaints of fraud were among the most frequent ones made.) In all economic dealing outside the household, altering of appearances to enhance apparent value is common procedure. The buyer, the trader, or the employer assumes he must constantly be on guard to protect himself, lest he suffer an engaño at the hands of someone more skilled in deception. Ixtepejanos assume that much of what one encounters in life is not "legitimate," but is *falso* (false), or a *mentira* (lie), or an engaño. Appearances are deceiving, one can never be sure when a supposedly trusted person or object may turn out to be false, and to betray a trust. These experiences are *ilusiones* (illusions).

An *ilusión* is any disappointment in which an apparently desirable state of affairs turns out in reality to be disastrous. This theme, and in particular the phrase *mis ilusiones* are recurrent in popular songs and poetry. (Engaño is more common as a folk tale motif.) It is also a frequent dream theme. For example, a young woman reported the following dream several months before her marriage:

Last night I dreamt that I got married, but I don't remember who the husband was. There was a wedding fiesta; then my husband died and I remained a widow.

Another woman says:

Last Monday I dreamt that I found a great quantity of ancient money. I tried to get it in the pockets of my apron and then piled it in my shawl. I was very scared from having found it and was very anxious to find a place to hide it. Then I discovered that it was too old to spend.

The following dream, also a woman's, contains the common theme of a desirable object close at hand, but unobtainable:

Before my little daughter died, the Virgin of the Rosary appeared to me. She was suspended in the sky. She was very bright and had a necklace of shining yellow stones. She was very beautiful and I almost succeeded in kissing her. Then I realized she had come to take my daughter.

A man dreamt:

I was reaching out to grab a beautiful clump of wheat; as I put my hand around it, it turned into an ugly snake.

Since social deception is endemic and much of life is illusionary, man, to defend himself, must constantly test appearances. The next chapter discusses the testing of social reality; here we shall examine attitudes about the nonsocial world.

Ixtepejanos are pragmatic people; they assume that material things are intrinsically more valuable than abstract things. For one reason, it is easier to test the appearances of physical objects than abstractions such as ideas and ideals. Therefore, greater credence is given to material things. An example will demonstrate this. Micaela, a woman living in El Cerezal, came to see the doctor in the municipio because of stomach pains. He sent her to Oaxaca City for an X-ray examination that revealed she had a tumor of the uterus requiring surgery. Rafael, the doctor, repeatedly told her of the seriousness of her condition, but since the pains were bearable she was not willing to have the operation. One day as he was going to Oaxaca City he stopped to see her. By chance he had with him the X-ray, and showed it to Micaela. Upon seeing the shadow in the film, the tumor suddenly became a reality to her, something that was actually there and had to be removed. She decided at that moment to have the operation. This incident is not surprising considering the common curing practice of sucking out foreign objects that have entered the body, causing some ailment. *Curanderos* who perform this service are acting in accord with the idea that material things are more credible than nonmaterial things. In other words, the foreign object removed from the flesh and shown to the patient is demonstrable proof of the cure. The same logic applies in the similar practice of rubbing the body with eggs so that foreign matter will pass into the egg and can be seen when the egg is broken open.

Also significant here is that in Ixtepeji each saint is represented—actually said to exist—in a material form. God is one exception, for there is no image of Him and therefore his whereabouts are uncertain. But where are the saints? "Obviously they are in the church; you can see them there."

Ixtepejanos place little value on pure knowledge since it is useless in a world of illusions. And some informants point out that studying may actually cause insanity. For example, reading the Bible is the reason given for the "insane" behavior of Protestant converts. (This explanation may have been suggested by the Catholic

Construction of adobe house.

Placing adobe brick in place.

clergy's opposition to Bible study.) Other people are also said to have become demented from too much school work.

Aesthetic criteria are based on functional utility and material worth rather than on some abstract notion of beauty. Hendry similarly describes the aesthetic sensibilities of the potters of Atzompa in the Valley. "In daily life pottery is rarely judged on artistic merit. When the Atzopeños buy the loza, or make it for their own use, they never choose the decorative ware, though they may think it 'looks prettier,' more essential considerations enter in, chiefly economic ones as the loza fina is more expensive. Along with price, the other factor of importance to them is function" (Hendry 1957:249). Similarly, in Ixtepeji things are "beautiful" because they are well-made and wear well. Rarely do carpenters, masons, or other craftsmen mention aspects of design or other abstract qualities such as form or color as being significant criteria of a good piece of work.

Most Ixtepejanos pray regularly, usually to a particular saint. "To pray," in Ixtepeji, means "to ask" (*pedir*), and prayers are usually requests for food, money, health, and general protection for the individual and his family. This pattern is in accord with Parsons' observation that in Mitla, prayers are for material benefits, for health, long life, crops, wealth, and for revenge, and that "ideas of moral or spiritual welfare are negligible" (1936:511). Leslie also notes that as far as he could determine, Mitleños, "did not pray for supernatural help to achieve a more virtuous life" (1960:50).

The extent to which Ixtepejanos see the world as illusion often becomes apparent when speaking with informants about abstract ideas. Often they turn the tables and, in genuine puzzlement, ask the ethnographer, who by virtue of being an "experienced outsider" should know such things, "What is the truth; what are we to believe?"

7

Thou Shalt Covet

ENVY OF THE RELATIVE good fortune of others is a strong theme in Latin American society. To cause envy in another person is potentially to incur attack by him, often by witchcraft. Therefore, there are many culturally prescribed defensive patterns to limit instilling envy in others (Foster 1965a). This chapter examines how envy and several related folk concepts affect interpersonal relations in Ixtepeji.[1]

Muina and Chípil

The folk concepts of *muina* and *chípil,* which are pervasive in Mesoamerica, are prominent in Ixtepeji. Muina is a psychogenic ailment that most commonly results from envy or anger. The crucial factor in its formation is that there is no readily available means to dissipate the engendered emotional energy. Without distorting the folk beliefs we may say that when expression of negative emotion is frustrated it is directed inward, into the person who has the envy or anger. Muina has the same effects on the heart and blood as *susto.* Both poison the blood, which in turn poisons the body and causes the heart to swell. The effects of susto, however, are usually transitory, while those of muina are cumulative and may eventually result in permanent physical deformities, such as the neck and head bent over on the shoulder and stiffened in this position, hunchback, and, in extreme cases, paralysis, especially of the arms. Although both similarly affect the blood, when a person is *asustado,* he blanches, whereas muina causes him to turn red with a feeling of hotness in the head as the blood rises. An inevitable symptom of muina is loss of appetite which, for various reasons discussed below, the afflicted person usually attempts to conceal. Also, there is the belief that eating or drinking while

---

[1] Rubel (1966) describes the importance of envy in determining social interaction in a Mexican–American community that is similar in this respect to Ixtepeji.

Young girls of Ixtepeji.

one has muina further poisons the blood. For example, Pablo Ocampo explained what happened to Aurelio Medellin who had died recently by saying that, "After he ate breakfast his mother started to scold him (a common cause of muina) because he had not brought a turkey from Oaxaca. Later in the street he met a friend who invited him for some mezcal. The mezcal after the breakfast and with the muina poisoned his blood and killed him."

Some informants occasionally refer to muina as *la bilis*, meaning "gall" or "anger," and apparently confuse it with the appendix. As one informant described it, *"La bilis* is *la muina.* It's a part that we have in the stomach, in the left side, like a finger. When one gets mad, it gets big and attacks us with a pain in the stomach. It's always because of muina. We go to the doctors for this sometimes since it is part of the body, but they give little relief. Usually people cure better with *curanderos.* If they don't cure, they die." The extent to which muina is a consciously thought of folk concept used to explain human motivation is hard to overemphasize.

While individuals of any age may suffer from muina, chípil is a disease of infants and children. This folk concept broadly translated is "sibling rivalry." More specifically, it is a special instance of envy on the part of the next to the youngest child toward the youngest, both pre- and postnatally. Its folk etiology is both organic and psychogenic. It is believed that the *chipiloso* is poisoned by the mother's milk because she is sick due to the *zocoyote* or *zocoyota*, which she has inside her. For this reason, weaning usually occurs with recognition of the mother's next pregnancy. (This is another instance of early childhood experience or rejection.) But more generally chípil is believed to result from envy because the younger child is usurping attention and affection that the mother formerly fostered on the chipiloso (*cf.* Foster 1965b).

Children become consciously aware of chípil as well as deception (Chapter 6) at an early age. The general consequence of this is that the child does not develop a strong sense of confidence in his parents; he has been taught that they are unpredictable and cannot always be relied on to supply nurture and security. As regards his siblings, he comes to realize that he is in direct competition with them for the favors of the mother. This early cognizance of chípil and the use of deception is illustrated by the following: Victoria wanted her baby Alejandro to come to her so she could change his shirt, as he had spilled lamp oil on the one he was wearing. She told young Alicia to bring him. Instead of going to Alejandro she went to her mother and sitting on the floor next to her pretended to suck at her breast. When Alejandro saw this, he immediately toddled to his mother and pushed in against her, crowding away Alicia who appeared quite self-satisfied with her trick.

The symptoms of chípil are similar to muina, but less pronounced, and are usually transitory. And, although chípil is never attributed to adults, muina is often associated with chípil in children. For example, when Alicia, a chipilosa aged four, has muina for whatever reasons, members of the family and especially her mother refer to her as *La Chipilosa* or *La Chipi* and often make fun of her. Such a sequence often starts with her aggravating her mother or someone else, usually by playing roughly with her one-and-a-half-year-old brother causing him to cry. The women will then often cuddle and give him much attention, while temporarily ignoring

Alicia, during which time she tries to break into the sphere of affection and attention. After a while, a small push or poke by one of the other older children causes
her to break into tears. This in turn evokes a barrage of ridicule by her mother and
older sisters whereupon her crying turns to quiet sobbing or whimpering while
she dejectedly retreats into a dark corner where she cannot be seen, but where she
is still the target of occasional remarks tossed out from the bustle and attention
centering on the baby: "Is Alicia angry?" "Does she have muina?" "Yes, she's a
very angry one." "Where did the chipilosa go?"

Children react to such mocking similarly to the way they react to being
whipped or harshly scolded. Such events are inevitably followed by the child's
withdrawing to some inconspicuous place; at such times he or she will often find
some object toward which to direct the now heightened muina. One day there was
a commotion in Doña Gregoria's patio. She was beating her twelve-year-old son,
Bartolo, with a broomstick, while screaming at him that he was lazy, only wanted
to play and not take care of the *tienda*, and that he did not care about her. Bartolo
was sitting on the ground where she had thrown him down, and was passively
receiving the full force of the blows with no attempt to protect himself. When
Gregoria had vented her anger she retired to her kitchen where she continued to
scold Bartolo who quietly went about his chores in a morose manner atypical of
him. About half an hour later Bartolo went to feed a bucket of corn to a pig tied
nearby. The way he usually did this daily chore was casually to throw the contents
of the pail on the ground and depart. But this time he set the pail on the ground,
and as the pig strained on its rope to reach the pail, Bartolo grabbed rocks and
clods from the ground and viciously threw them at the animal. Then taking the
pail and throwing its contents on the pig, he gave it several hard kicks accompanied
by a string of profanities.

The next example follows the same pattern as the above: One afternoon
little Lucila burst into tears in front of the Ibarra house where the children were
playing. She said Lupe had bitten her and Ramona went out to see. Paying no attention to Lucila, she went to where Lupe was sitting on the ground, and taking up
a rope gave her a lashing on her back and bare legs. Lupe made no move to defend
herself and only turned her face away from the flailing rope. Ramona then came
back to the kitchen telling Lupe what a bad child she was. Meanwhile Lupe, sobbing
softly, went out into the street behind the house and proceeded to pull small plants
out of a rock wall and tear them apart.

Such suppression of emotion is not only typical of children with muina.
One afternoon two women, Manuela and Ramona, were chatting while Francisca,
age sixteen, was working silently around the cooking fire. After a while she went
and stood in the kitchen door, leaning on the door post and gazing out into the
patio for a moment. Then the family's small crippled dog, who for the last four
months had been recovering from severe wounds, limped by. Without warning,
Francisca gave him a tremendous kick in the side which flung him from the stoop.
She then walked off without a word, while Manuela began to scold her for such a
cruel act, making the distinction between the normal way of kicking dogs and this
kind which results from muina, ending with the usual, *"es muy enojona,"* which
translates roughly as, "She's easily angered and prone to muina."

On another morning a woman neighbor came to the Ibarra house. She was given bread and chocolate as she explained that she came to borrow some ink to put on a burn one of her children got the night before when an older brother knocked a pitcher of hot coffee off the hearth onto the smaller child. After she left, the Ibarras speculated that the older child burned the smaller one intentionally, *por muina,* and compared this incident with how Francisca, several years before, burned her younger sister Marta with a flatiron. Pánfilo gave an energetic reenactment of how Francisca, while ironing, pushed the flatiron aggressively back and forth and finally shoved it onto Marta's leg. Francisca is considered to be very *enojona* by the rest of the family and frequently gets teased about it, a practice which in turn angers her more.

The Social Meaning of Food Sharing

The offering and receiving of food is perhaps the most fundamental economic and ritual act in human society. One variant of this exchange behavior is particularly conspicuous to the anthropologist doing fieldwork in rural Oaxaca and

Boy in the doorway of a kitchen.

in other peasant societies. It is the insistent offering of some food or drink by a host to a stranger or casual acquaintance upon his entry into the home, and the virtually unavoidable obligation of the guest to partake. Here we will examine this custom and present an explanation that accounts for its strength. Although the data come primarily from Ixtepeji, the explanation applies to rural Mexico in general.

In Ixtepeji, when a guest enters a home, a representative of the host family offers him something to eat or drink, which he will then decline until he is eventually coaxed, or finally forced, to accept.[2] Outside the home similar coercions are also applied to induce reluctant individuals to accept alcohol (Chapter 10). To give an indication of the strength of these pressures to participate, suffice it to say that I have collected accounts of men being shot for refusing to accept a drink. Although my own life has never been so imperiled, on a number of occasions I have had a sore arm from the vise-like grip of acquaintances who forcibly insisted that I eat and drink at their invitation.

Among existing theories of food exchange we find none that explain this particular kind of host–guest interaction, especially the insistence with which food is pressed upon the guest and his sense of obligation to consume it on the spot.[3] At present there are two theoretical approaches to the social psychology of food sharing; we may refer to them as the commensualism and the genetic theories. Proponents of commensualism theory argue that there is some cohesive social function inherent in the act of communal eating, or that somehow the individual perceives that eating in the presence of others is of potential magical benefit to him (Richards 1964:174–182). According to genetic theory a proclivity to share or not to share food arises from the cultural patterning of the child's physiological dependence on its mother and other members of the family, rather than from inherent social functions or in magic beliefs (Richards 1964:212–213). Cohen (1961) presented an interesting genetic argument about personality and world view formation being dependent on early gratification experiences. In short, he says that consistent gratification of hunger on demand, "instills within the maturing infant a world view predicated on the notion that there is enough food in the world, that one can always secure food when one needs it, and that other persons will give food when asked for it" (Cohen 1961:325). By similar reasoning he hypothesizes that food deprivation in infancy and early childhood predisposes the individual to perceive "himself as an inadequate person, specifically, a hungry and impoverished one. Just as the individual views himself as one who 'never has enough'—and this impression is inescapable in the 'nonsharing' societies —so does he view the world as 'not having enough *for* him'" (Cohen 1961:326).

On the basis of Cohen's argument and the following outline of Ixtepeji world view and economy, one would logically suspect that food sharing would be greatly attenuated in Ixtepeji. But it is precisely there with a world view of

---

[2] Hammel (1967:59) describes a similar pattern in Serbia where the women of a household coerce guests to eat, but in Ixtepeji men are as adamant in offering food as are women.

[3] An exception to this occurs in more Indian, as opposed to mestizo, areas of southern Mexico where, although there are also strong pressures to accept offered alcohol, the guest may, however, pour it into his own bottle for later consumption.

general deprivation, or "image of diminishing good" (Kearney 1969:889), that the pattern of food sharing under discussion appears so intensely.

By showing that there are reasons to share food other than those summarized above, I do not imply that the various explanations are contradictory. One could make a good case for commensualism theory by looking at eating patterns at fiestas and other ceremonial occasions in Ixtepeji (*cf.* Chapter 12). Also, a good case for Cohen's second genetic hypothesis can be made; Ixtepeji children often go hungry and, aside from the particular pattern of food sharing described here, Ixtepejanos prefer to eat in the seclusion of the nuclear family's kitchen. There is also much secrecy and tension surrounding food and economic resources in general. Therefore, a search for the most parsimonious explanation can thus distort, by oversimplification, the intricacies of so complex a behavioral trait as food sharing. The very strength of this social pattern in Ixtepeji is in large part explained by the varied levels of explanation that we must bring to bear on it; there are psychological, social, and cultural forces maintaining it.

Although Ixtepejanos live at a higher level of economic security than the Siriono of Bolivia, for example, for whom Holmberg (1960) has shown that food anxieties significantly affect behavioral and cultural forms, there is still much anxiety about subsistence. Ixtepejanos perceive themselves as precariously dependent on an effete and harsh environment. Although few people experience continuous hunger, many do go hungry occasionally. The possession of meager or no capital resources to fall back on in time of need adds to this basic food anxiety, which in turn affects world view and social interaction.

As for the food itself, there are relatively few basic dishes, although they vary from one kitchen to another. But if the cuisine is simple, attitudes and feelings about it are not. Strongest among these are feelings about foods from one's natal area. Nowhere else is the food as good, and in that region the food of one's own town is the best, and the best cook in that town is of course one's own mother or wife. Men in particular are concerned about having proper food to fortify themselves for manual labor. The crucial staple here is corn, which to be effective must be eaten as *tortillas*. A meal without tortillas is in effect not a meal. Even though gorged, a man is apt to say that the meal "did not give me satisfaction," if tortillas are lacking.

Communal drinking of the three locally used alcoholic beverages (*mezcal, tepache,* and beer) is in some respects a special variation of the food-sharing pattern (*cf.* Chapter 10). Here we can mention several motives to share alcohol; the first is expressed in folk belief. Ixtepejanos themselves are ready to explain that a man or group of men who are drinking are insistent that all men present drink with them so that no one will be more sober and so be in a position to take advantage of the drinkers. But after observing interaction in such settings another reason becomes apparent, which does not necessarily contradict this folk explanation. As described earlier, there is a great deal of suppressed hostility in interpersonal relations in Ixtepeji. For the most part hostility is not openly expressed but comes out in disguised form and surreptitious attack, often under the guise of kindness. In accord with this pattern, the presentation of food and drink is on the surface a kindly gesture, but when it is pressed upon an unwilling recipient (who as we shall see has reasons compelling him to accept it), it becomes a hostile act calculated to inconvenience the guest.

A psychologically related dimension that also enters in here is that of masculine honor and respect. The same was true in ancient Gaul and Germany and turn of the century France where among farmers and students one was obliged "to swallow quantities of liquid to 'do honour' in grotesque fashion to the host" (Mauss 1967:40). Similarly in Ixtepeji, to refuse an invitation to drink is usually tantamount to a direct insult. That men can be and are insulted by a refusal to accept a drink (refusal to accept food is not usually such a strong insult) seems, however, more bound up with the psychology of *machismo* than with food sharing per se and so I mention it here only in passing.

Let us now look at the other main oral activity—talking—for folk ideas about it are relevant to patterns of food sharing. Ixtepejanos are talkative people. Talking is an important part of social interaction and one gets the definite impression that Ixtepejanos are more concerned with the manner and content of speech than, for example, Anglo–Americans. Why should this be so? What other function besides direct communication can language be serving? Here it is to be noted that it is not talking per se that is valued, but rather talking done by individuals. This is to say that the kind of talking that most interests Ixtepejanos is another's speech that is addressed directly to the individual. Other patterns of speaking such as an individual addressing a formal group or addressing several people at once are not necessarily of interest and are often considered an annoyance. In their concern with paralinguistic aspects of speech Ixtepejanos are especially attentive to cues revealing the emotional state of the person with whom they are speaking. This is understandable in view of certain folk beliefs, most importantly the concept of *muina*.

As we have seen, we can speak of muina as suppressed hostility. Furthermore, it is believed that muina, because it is not expressed, poisons the person's blood, which in turn may cause severe physical disabilities. Also, food eaten by a person who has muina aggravates the condition and may cause death. The main cause of muina is envy (*envidia*), which, besides causing muina, creates a desire to attack, most likely by witchcraft, the person who is envied. Therefore, a person who is known to have muina is potentially dangerous, and defensive measures against him, also probably by witchcraft, are in order.[4] Similarly, the person who has the muina acts on the same logic and attempts to conceal it, and so avoid a counterattack. He does this either by withdrawing from interaction with others, or by feigning normal behavior. Two of the main symptoms are loss of appetite and an unwillingness to talk. Therefore, to conceal muina, a person who has it will also sometimes force himself to eat and to talk, despite the harmful effects eating may have.[5] But since such behavior is forced and not natural, it can be detected by

---

[4] Reference here is to attitudes about the causes and frequency of witchcraft rather than the actual incidence of witchcraft attacks.

[5] Rubel (1966:166) relates how a Mexican–American woman informant in Texas gave as a cause of *empacho*, forcing oneself to eat something not desired in someone else's home so as to not offend the host. This explanation (not offending the host) for forcing oneself to eat offered food is one level of folk explanation often given in Ixtepeji and does not logically contradict the *muina* explanation which, as with all subjects touching on witchcraft, is much less likely to be mentioned by informants.

a discerning observer. How does one detect muina in another? As one informant put it, "The only way to tell if a person has it, is to notice how they look at you and speak to you. If they are very short with you or give you some ugly glances, you note these things." From this point of view, individual to individual speech allows a person to determine if another person is possibly harboring evil intent toward him. An exchange of muina-free speech over a bowl of beans or a bottle of mezcal assures each one that at least for the time being he has no cause to fear his companion.[6]

From the individual's point of view then, openness and naturalness are desirable qualities in others, but to behave in this manner oneself involves certain double binds. On one hand he wants to present an image of himself as open and without muina, whether he has it or not. To be suspected of having it is to be defined as dangerous and to be avoided and retaliated against. But on the other hand, this demonstration of being free of muina goes against another desired mode of self-defense, namely concealment of any good fortune that one may be experiencing.[7] Thus a balance must be struck between two conflicting ideal modes of presenting oneself to others in everyday life: One must convince others that he himself is free of muina; that is, he must appear open and content, but he must do this in a manner such that he does not reveal his real state of being. That is, if he is really content, he must not let on that he is lest he incur another's envy.

A good deal of social interaction in Ixtepeji involves individuals managing impressions of themselves so as to strike a compromise in the above dilemma. Although such behavior is impossible to quantify, it appears that rather than trying to strike an even balance between the two, Ixtepejanos attempt to give the impression that they are worse off than they really are. To this end they also often present themselves in a self-disparaging manner.[8] With these social strategies and attitudes about speech and muina in mind we can now discuss how they affect food sharing. Let us proceed by analyzing an incident that took place in Ixtepeji.

One morning a vendor selling pitchers and chiles came into Doña Paulina's patio. Paulina bought nothing, explaining that she had no money, but she did invite the man, a complete stranger, to have some food, which he accepted and ate in her kitchen. After he left, I asked Paulina if he would be given something to eat in most of the houses that he entered. She said "No," because very few people "know how to be good people." She explained how persons, like this man, who were traveling into strange towns often had nothing to eat but a cold tortilla because they had no friends and no one invited them to eat. She said that she felt sorry for such people and that it was the duty of people who had food and were eating to share it in such cases, since to do so was the sign of a good person. She went on at length with this theme and then casually remarked that sometimes such people who *were not* invited to eat in such circumstances later did *maldades*, or "evil things," to the person who did not invite them in. She also told how potentially

---

[6] It is interesting but not necessarily significant that *compañero* and related words such as the English "companion" derive from the Latin *com* (with) and *panis* (bread) and originally denoted someone with whom bread was shared.

[7] *Cf.* Foster (1965a), re "the Principle of Equivalence."

[8] *Cf.* Cleaveland and Longaker (1957:170–171, 184–194).

dangerous such strangers were and how they frightened her, and that she always gave them something to eat "to be safe."[9] She told how she always explained to such people that she was very poor and only had a few tortillas and beans in the kitchen, but that they were welcome to what she had. She further explained how she was going to keep a large basket full of tortillas during the fiesta in the coming month since there would be many pilgrims and vendors—many strangers—coming to her house.

In this instance Paulina herself well articulates the logic of her actions. She expresses the common theme that the man who came to her house was a stranger, an unknown person, and therefore someone to beware of since such people are potentially dangerous in this capacity alone. But in this case, such a person is doubly dangerous since he came to the house while those inside were eating, which is something he could be envious of if he were arriving with an empty stomach. To prevent this Paulina does two things. First, she shares food with the stranger, and second, she attempts to create the impression that she is really very poor and not worthy of his envy. Also, since one of the symptoms of muina and envy is loss of appetite and desire to talk, offering food to the man is a test of whether or not he bears ill feelings. Insisting that a visitor eat thus accomplishes two things. First, it lessens the possibility of engendering envy; and second, provides an opportunity to observe nuances in the visitor's speech and general behavior, which are indications of his emotional state.

The above example is a variation on a common Latin American pattern that is acted out whenever an outsider to a family group comes on the scene during a meal. In Ixtepeji this compulsion to feed outsiders is not limited to strangers, but also applies to close friends and relatives, who are in close contact with an individual and are therefore in a position to know his personal state of affairs. Intimate knowledge of this kind has two implications. It may be a source of envy and muina, and it also allows for more effective aggression, which the envy and muina provoke. Intimates and relatives are thus equated with strangers as the potentially most dangerous category of people. In contrast, it is acquaintances in the midrange of familiarity who are the least threatening, that is, those with whom one interacts enough so that he can discern something of their general state of being, but yet not enough so that they can deeply penetrate into his own inner state or economic situation.[10] As with strangers and intimates, the emotional state of persons in this category is also assessed by astute observation of their eating, speech, and general demeanor.

Various anthropological theories about systems of reciprocity have looked at them in psychological and functional terms to analyze their integrative and adaptive functions. What I have said here is not contrary to these approaches, but

---

[9] The possibility that the stranger was bringing "cold air" into her house did not enter her thinking in this instance, although, in accord with notions of disease etiology stemming from the Hippocratic humoral theory, this is a common concern throughout Mexico.

[10] This midrange of intimacy is institutionalized, for example, in *compadrazgo* relationships, which often entail a shift to a formal relationship, expressed among other ways in a change from an informal *tu* form of address to the formal *usted*. The implication of this seems to be that where it is desirable that relationships be functional for long periods of time, they are best maintained at the midrange of intimacy where there is less chance for emotional disruptions.

instead demonstrates that exchange, in this case the exchange of food and speech, may also be looked at from another angle. In Ixtepeji, at least, an invitation or insistence upon sharing food and a few moments of conversation is more than a fulfilling of reciprocal obligations. It is also a means of social self-defense and reality testing.

8

The Passage of Time

T HE WAY in which people conceive of time and the values they attach to it
are culturally determined. The following paragraphs describe how Ixtepejanos regard various temporal orders and some implications of these basic
assumptions. This treatment is short since much of the relevant material pertains
to Proposition number 5 (Chapter 4), and is presented in the next chapter.

Historic and Cosmic Time

In terms of "Variations in Value-Orientations" theory there are three possible cultural interpretations of the human temporal focus: Past, Present, and
Future (Kluckhohn and Strodtbeck 1961:13–15). In Ixtepeji the rank ordering
of variation in Time Orientation is Past> Present> Future.[1] In accordance with
Proposition number 4, Ixtepejanos believe that the historic past was better than
the present, and the present is better than the future will be. In short, they believe
that their living conditions are deteriorating. Myth and folklore, and ruins of old
buildings and mines testify that former times were more prosperous, that the soil
was more fertile, and the weather milder. Men remark that crops are now less
abundant, that one must go further from town for firewood, and that there is less
gentle rain and more frost.

Ixtepejanos believe that, not only in the local environment but also in the
world at large, the forces of entropy and destruction are winning. This process will
eventually end in *el día de justicia* (the Judgment Day), when the world will end
in a fiery cataclysm—the ultimate catastrophe.

In addition to believing that the environment is becoming less bountiful,

---

[1] Based in part on analysis of the "Time Orientation," in a slightly altered Spanish Language
version of the Value-Orientation Schedule (Kluckhohn and Strodtbeck 1961:368–378).
N=25.

Collecting firewood in woods above town.

many Ixtepejanos believe that they as a race are deteriorating. To demonstrate how robust his ancestors were in comparison to the present population Don Sebastián told how he discovered an ancient Zapotec tomb, and produced a large *mano* (grinding stone) he had found in it. "Look at the size of this stone," he said. "It would take two of our women to use it!"

Concepts of Aging

Human processes of growth and aging, and human life force, are thought of in the same manner as are the analogous phenomena in the nonhuman world. This is demonstrated in forms of speech. Old people, for example, often employ such usages as, "Thanks to God I still have enough force to defend myself in life." "God is giving me force to work a little while longer." "God is still lending me life." Such phrases express related themes: 1) Life is granted arbitrarily by an uncomprehended power that can reclaim it at any time. It is as though life were loaned for a while, but must be paid back on demand, that is, when God wishes to recollect it. There is a commonly used simile with harvesting here: God sows souls and reaps the harvest. 2) Life (the self) must be defended from aggressive and exploitive forces which also surround and constantly threaten crops and animals. 3) Life is a vital force that enters the body and animates it; this force is expended like the fertility of the soil, or like fuel, and the body dies when it is drained (*agotado*) of this force. To be old is also to be tired (*cansado*), which is how overworked land is described. This sentiment is well expressed in a popular

Charcoal oven ready for firing.

Mexican song, ". . . *hay una tormenta que nos roba poco a poco alma, vida, y corazón.*"[2]

     Aging, dying, and natural sickness are all thought of as resulting from a loss of this vital life force. When this happens a person becomes weak and loses endurance, or *resistencia*. Physically this is noticeable by a loss of weight. It is for this reason that there is a premium placed on more corpulant body types, usually referred to as *macizo*. Although Ixtepejanos disparage obesity, they express a preference for being heavy. One day, Don Sebastián, as he lay on his death bed, uncovered his thin limbs to demonstrate how sick and weak he was. He talked of how he no longer had force to work his lands as he used to, and compared growing old to a plant dying, *se acaba,* when its sap and its "force" are drained out and it weakens and shrivels up. "When one is young he is strong and solid, but one drains out." Another philosophical old man expressed this same idea by saying, "One passes like a *milpa*, thus pass the people, like this young child here. They are born little and start growing and in a little while they give *elote*. And then they get more solid and give *mazorca*, and later *maíz*—something one can eat. And then arrives the hour that they dry up and no longer have *naturaleza*. Such is life."

     The life force is necessary if a person is to have endurance and be able to work. But it can be lost, drained away, from sickness and overwork. For this reason, periodic rest is needed, at least once a week, when man and beast can be replenished. This thinking is parallel to the idea of passage through the civil–religious hierarchy: One bears a *cargo* for a period, and then is allowed a rest for replenishment of resources and energy.

---

[2] ". . . there is a tempest that robs from us, little by little, our soul, life, and heart."

Woman in doorway of house constructed of rubble from buildings destroyed in 1912.

Many Ixtepejanos fear growing old, especially if they have few or no children or close relatives. Although relieved of community obligations, old people are also expected to relinquish wealth and authority to younger relatives, who are responsible for their welfare. Should one be fortunate enough to have devoted sons and daughters, old age can be a time of relative leisure, but even so, many old people resent the attendant lowering of their status. Without children to work one's lands, old age can be a time of extreme hardship. One old man living alone with his wife described the plight of the old by saying,

> We are turned loose like animals; no one pays any attention to us. We are outside of the law; we are completely abandoned, and no one but God helps us. Since we had no crop this year because of the heavy rains we are just living off our few trees and chickens. We work just to live and to wait for the grace of God, but who knows what day it will arrive. God put us in the world and he removes us too. Only he knows where we go next. When God doesn't like something he removes it all. What is one to do? Several years ago I had seven head of cattle, but God took them all. It's a chore to live here in the world without children.

Life is difficult on earth, but conditions do not improve after death. All that remains of a deceased individual is a shadow-like spirit. Disembodied spirits are invariably in a less desirable state after death than before. At death the spirit must enter into the *aire*, a gaseous solitude (*soledad*) from which there is no escape. As such it is deprived of the pleasures and security that the living can have, but at the same time it is not released from the sufferings and longings that it had when alive. Ixtepejanos do not, therefore, see life after death as a desirable alternative to the harsh realities of life on earth. This reasoning perhaps explains the absence of suicide in Ixtepeji.

Another implication of the above mentioned rank ordering of the Time

Elderly Ixtepejano.

Elderly couple of Ixtepeji.

Orientation is that Ixtepejanos tend to exploit resources in the present rather than conserving them for an uncertain future. Since they regard the future as unpredictable (e.g., there are no folk techniques for telling fortunes), and tending to worsen, it is rational to avail oneself of all desirable things when they are at hand. They assume it is better to pick fruit before it is ripe, rather than wait for something to happen to it, just as it makes good sense to avail oneself of natural resources before someone else does. This desire to maximize in the present with little regard for the future is an obstacle to attempts at conservation of natural resources and community development. Development by definition implies a faith in and positive value of the future. Accordingly, informants tell how a representative of the Federal Ejidal Program came several years ago and started planning for a federal credit and technical aid program. He collected much data, made many speeches on what was to be done, and aroused everyone's hopes. Then one day he left to report to Mexico, and was not seen again. Everyone became very disillusioned and sad. Some people seemed to relate this story as a way of politely saying they held no hopes that any study or programs would ever have practical results.

Speech Patterns and Time Orientation

Unbroken continuity of conversation is not valued; people are not disturbed when the flow of a conversation is interrupted. If two or more people are engaged in a dialogue and another wishes to interject a comment or speak to one of those present, he will most likely interrupt the speaker, providing status and prestige considerations are such as to allow this action. That is, the interrupter must be roughly the equal or superior of the speaker, except in the case of children to whom no such restrictions apply. The power of an interrupter to arrest the flow of talk is striking. Likely as not, it will come in the middle of a sentence that is immediately cut-off by the speaker as attention centers on the new speaker who has until then not been in the conversation. The train of conversation is then usually picked up again as soon as the interruption has ended.

Interruptions are rarely of such a nature as to change the course of a conversation; they are far more apt to be totally irrelevant items. Once they are taken care of, the speaker will resume where he left off. However, unlike the common pattern in the United States, the speaker will not interject some comment such as, "Let's see, where was I?" or "I wish I wasn't always interrupted"; rather, the thread of the conversation is taken up with no concern for the fact that the flow of talk was momentarily cut off. This immediate turning of attention to an interruption is most evident in the case of children as interrupters. And, again in contrast to the United States, children are rarely admonished for interrupting; instead, the conversation ceases and they are given full attention.

The lack of concern over interruptions is in accord with a relatively non-linear and predominantly present time-orientation. In other words, conversation is not conceived of as existing through time in the sense of developing from A through B to C. There is thus no concern over a break in such a nonexistent continuity; all that matters is that communication occurs. Similarly, the acceptance and focusing of attention on interruptions is in accord with a present orientation in that an interruption is something occurring *now*, and as such merits immediate attention.

These observations which indicate a dominant present time orientation are supported by the Spanish grammatical usage, common in Ixtepeji, of indicating probability, doubt, and conjecture in the present by use of the future tense. Since the future is seen as uncertain, unpredictable, and undependable, it is logically consistent to indicate doubt and conjecture in the present by use of the future tense and all that thought of the future implies. Furthermore, this usage most often has an element of anxiety associated with it as well. For example, the phrase *¿Quién será ese hombre que viene?* translates as "Who will this man be who is coming now (in the present)?" and expresses a certain uneasiness about an approaching stranger.

These related behavioral traits indicate a tendency to give emphasis to the present rather than a perceived, inherently uncertain, and, in all probability, less desirable future. These sentiments are succinctly expressed in the proverb, *Hoy somos y mañana no sabemos,* which may be translated as "We are here alive and well today, but who knows what undesirable turn of events tomorrow will bring." This is a parallel usage in Ixtepeji of the phrase *estamos sin novedad* (literally, "we are without new event"), which is used, especially in letters, to convey the idea that no harm has befallen the speaker and his family. The implicit assumption here seems to be that any novel occurrence would probably be for the worse.

9

The Burden of Life

PROPOSITION NUMBER 5 (Chapter 4) states that, "Hard work and suffering are inevitable consequences of life." Life in Ixtepeji is seen as a constant struggle for survival. This view is expressed in commonly uttered phrases such as, *Voy a hacer la lucha a* . . . ("I am going to make the struggle to . . ."), and *Estoy luchando la vida* (literally, "I am struggling with life"; "I am surviving"). Life is a struggle in the sense that it is seen as full of burdens one must bear.

A subjective idea of this major attitude toward life is suggested by the following supposedly true story told by a middle-aged man, who used it to explain why it is important to make proper arrangements, on All Souls' Day, for the spirits of dead relatives.

> This story is about a man who had to be away from town for this celebration. Before leaving he diligently made all the necessary arrangements—prepared his altar, cleaned his house, and most importantly, baked special breads and raised money to buy food and drink. He gave the remaining money to his wife and put her in charge of seeing that the altar was properly set. His wife, however, was not a good woman and as soon as he left, she started to eat all the food until nothing was left to put on the altar for the dead. She became frightened and so she got a large rock and put it on the altar. Several nights later as her husband was returning home, he saw the spirits of his mother and father walking out of town. God gave him this momentary power so he would know what his wife had done. Each of his parents was carrying a large rock on their backs and was in great misery.

Attitudes toward Municipal *Cargos*

As in most small rural Mexican communities, local residents fill municipal office, or *cargos*, on a nonpaid basis. To say that they do so voluntarily would misrepresent strong attitudes about cargo service. These attitudes are similar to those that Cancian describes in Zinacantan. "The cargo must be a financial burden to the

Typical bread oven used in Sierra Juárez.

cargo holder, and he must accept this burden in good spirits, happy that he is sacrificing for the gods and the saints" (Cancian 1965:97). They are similar since all cargos in Ixtepeji are economic liabilities, literally and figuratively thought of as burdens diabolically inflicted on the individual by those who elect him. By the same token the period between cargos is an individual's *descanso*, or "rest." The similarity with the Zinacantan does not, however, extend to the acceptance of the cargo happily and in good spirits. Quite to the contrary, there is open and un-concealed attempt to avoid service and strongly voiced displeasure at having to serve. Pablo Martínez who three years before finished a term as *suplente de primer regidor* and now faces the prospect of another assignment, is not an outspoken man, yet he says "Nobody likes to fulfill cargos, we just don't like to do it. It is only by force that we are made to do it. The people who vote for a candidate are punishing us. It's a punishment. No one is there in the municipio for his own pleas-ure, but by force." Referring to the cargos he has fulfilled, his comments are all equivalent to, "They were all miserable," (for example, such phrases as *todos son malos y pesados*).

Ixtepejanos accept municipal cargos as unavoidable consequences of life in the town. The same attitudes pertain to work in general. The relation of work to leisure, which is a meaningful contrast in the United States, is virtually nonex-istent in Ixtepeji. It must be translated instead as an opposition between work and rest. Whereas in the United States, the absence of work is equivalent to leisure and is highly valued at certain times, the nonexistence of work does not exist as a category in the Ixtepeji concept of the world and the good life. Work—perennial and unremitting—is taken as a constant aspect of existence to such an extent that there is no speculation concerning its potential absence.

Religious Attitudes

Religious attitudes in Ixtepeji are typically Mexican with an emphasis on death and suffering. For example, Ixtepejanos identify with a Christ that embodies only certain of the attributes of the Christ of the complete Christian myth. The Christ of Ixtepeji suffered martyrdom, agony, and death without the benefits of divine ecstasy, wisdom, and triumph over death by ascension to heaven. All of the numerous images of Christ portray him, in realistic and gory detail, in some part of the Passion. Christ in Ixtepeji never has a halo; he is a Christ of Good Friday, but not Easter Sunday. A common sight in the church is a man praying on his knees with arms outstretched in the form of a crucifix for excruciatingly long periods of time. A folktale tells that when the church was sacked and the images of the saints stolen by the people of Ixtlán, an image of Christ became very heavy because he did not want to leave town, and the robbers were able to carry him only with great difficulty. Years later, when the town was resettled, a triumphant procession went to Ixtlán to reclaim Christ, at which time he was so light that he almost floated home. Often when this tale is told, an explicit analogy is made between this exile of Christ and that of the Ixtepejanos who suffered the same fate.

Sawing beams.

Fatalism

Ixtepejanos themselves explain the presence of suffering and struggle in terms of certain fatalistic concepts summed up in the term *destino* (destiny). A person is born with his own destino, which he cannot change; the most one can do is work to exploit its full potential. Beyond this absolute limit no amount of effort can improve the position of a person with a poor destino. This notion explains such things as why most people have to work "like animals," why there is poverty, why some people have no children, and so forth. It also explains personal characteristics. Why do some children do well in school, and from there go on to live comfortable lives? "Because they were so destined; other children can study day and night, but God does not give them this grace." Moral character is similarly a result of the destino a person is born with. There is, as usual, an appropriate saying about this, "Don't give the rope to the leopard." This means that if you have a son with a bad character you should not give him all the considerations you would a good son because he will abuse them, by squandering an inheritance or mistreating gifts, for example. Cenobio Peña, commenting on his own destiny, contrasts it with that of his two brothers. When they were all fighting in the north during the Revolution, it was their destino to be killed and eaten by coyotes and vultures, while his was to live and suffer more.

The fact that some people are rich and have special knowledge, and other advantages is accepted complacently, and explained by the concept of destiny. But

Washing clothes.

even the rich and wise must accord with their destinies, as many Ixtepejanos are quick to point out with a glint of satisfaction. As one man put it, "Those wise people are trying to get to the moon, but God isn't giving them permission to talk with it. Why are Americans so powerful? Because God gives them power. Their horses eat gasoline because God gives them this grace. These are things which in my stupidity I cannot understand." This same man continued to speak of local Protestants in the same vein, explaining why they say there is no God (which is a misinterpretation of what they in fact do say). "They say there is only nature. But if there were no Father how would we be here? Clearly there must be a God who rules the world. They say we are all brothers and equal, but one dies only when God disposes, like this flame [blowing out a stick taken from the fire to light a cigarette]; God disposes when he wants to."

The saints also have personal destinies, and in this respect differ from God. Neither Christ nor the other saints are capable of altering their destinies for, according to some but not all informants, they too are sinners who will be unable to escape the end of the world when it comes.

The concept of destino is closely related to a complex of personality and behavioral features that are suggested by the term "resignation." An example will show how these two concepts work together. On the afternoon after a frost, Aga-pito went to see some corn and beans he had planted. When he arrived his greatest fears were verified. Most of the *milpa*, still with young corn, was badly burned by the frost, but worse, a large area planted with beans was completely killed. He observed this scene with complete outer calm. The only negative emotion he ex-pressed was an occasional, *ni modos, ¿Qué voy a hacer?*, or *está jodido*, accompanied by a slackening of conversation. When he returned to the house, he did not volun-teer to tell the others of the disastrous event and only nonchalantly and casually described it to his father and mother when they asked him.

Although a person may be either positively or negatively destined, the concept of destino is almost always spoken of in relation to negative conditions and almost inevitably with a touch of ironic fatalism. For example, it is often said that there are rich gold veins under the town. In the words of one man, "Here we have treasures, but we are not able to move them. There are many riches here in the town, but for lack of money and since we don't know how, we can't get them. Someone from outside the country is necessary to get it started since they are wiser in these things and have money, unlike the Mexican government, which only cheats the people."

There are numerous folktales about treasures that have this ironic "so near, yet so far" quality. A well known one is about the enchanted cave, *llebasilli* (*cueva del río o cueva escondida*) which is near town.

> About twenty years ago, a man from La Cebollal heard an enchanted rooster in the rock where the cave is. He went to Oaxaca City and hired a spiritualist who said the spirit of the cave was ready to deliver the money that it guards there. The man then organized thirty men and started working in the cave. They worked like slaves for six months, when suddenly the cave filled with water. They then knew they were not destined to get the money and stopped working; to this day the money is still there under the water.

Another similar tale, which also has the theme of *engaño* woven into, it was told by Cipriano Ortega apparently with complete faith in its veracity:

> In another, earlier epoch, Montezuma brought the royal crown here. [A long description follows here about its size, heaviness, and value, probably suggested by the crown of the *Virgen de la Soledad* in Oaxaca.] Later the Spaniards took it to Spain. For this reason, Benito Juárez went to Spain to bring it back to his people. But he was not destined to do so. When he got to Spain, the army stopped him and took him to Queen Isabella in order to take his declaration, at which time he presented his law to her. She asked if the crown was really from Mexico. He said, "Yes, it is from my people, the Indians." [Another description is given here of the crown on a table in the middle of a large room lined with Spanish officers and nobles who were planning to kill Juárez.] Then the officers and nobles agreed that they would all attempt to put it on their heads and the first one who could do so would keep it. Juárez was to be the last. All the great men tried to lift it, but no one could. Then they said it was his turn. He put his blanket to one side and lifted the crown onto his head, and gave a turn around the room in front of all the Spaniards, thus proving it belonged to the Indians. They said they would give it to him to take home, but they poisoned him instead. He returned home dead.

Almost as pervasive as poverty in Cipriano's talk is the expression of the existence of engaño and uncertainty in the world. "We don't know what the truth is, this is why life is hard for us here in the world." He told of a friend who studied the Bible intensively for fifteen years and at the end still did not know what the "truth" was. There are other similar accounts of people who have gone crazy from studying. "How is one going to know what to think since we don't know the truth?" He speaks at length of how the Protestants are deceiving the people because they say they know what the truth is, and of how they are obviously lying since no one is capable of knowing it for certain. Always interspersed in such conversations are references to the way in which individuals are "destined." In one instance he used an analogy of one's living through, or dying in a battle as dependent on how one is destined. The image of a battle is indeed a fitting analogy to this view of life.

10

Everyone Must Drink

A

S IN MUCH, if not most, of rural Mexico, drunkenness is endemic in Ixtepeji. In Ixtepeji alcoholism frequently results in a specific syndrome, developing in middle-age men, which involves extreme personality and behavioral changes. This chapter discusses the epidemiology and symptomatology of this syndrome, related folk beliefs and practices, and the role of religious conversion as a means of escape from institutionalized social patterns compelling reluctant individuals to drink.

Folk Beliefs about Drinking

According to folk belief, an individual undergoes changes in personality while drinking because of the effects of the alcohol on the blood. The first stage is called *sangre de mono* or *sangre de chango* (monkey blood). A person in a state of sangre de chango is described as opening up; he "opens his confidence," becomes sentimental, and says things he does not ordinarily say. He is also apt to become uninhibited, friendly, and cavort about—thus the term "monkey blood." But as he continues, he passes into a stage of *sangre de león* (lion blood), which is induced by *tragos de valor*, or literally "swallows of valor." In this phase the drinker becomes belligerent, argumentative, and perhaps wants to fight; he drinks faster and soon enters the next stage of *sangre de cuche* (pig blood). He now loses control of his faculties, staggers, perhaps vomits, and eventually falls into a stupor, most likely to be left to lie where he has fallen. There is, of course, variation in the reactions of different individuals to alcohol; indeed, speaking in terms of the folk metaphor, some people are prone to behave more in accordance with one of the various types of sangre than another.

Usually when asked why one drinks or why there is so much drinking in the town, informants are at a loss to give an explanation. The most common response is that there is no other diversion, or that one talks better and rests better when intoxicated. Alcohol is also considered to have medicinal value and, according to folk medical beliefs, is prescribed for many minor ailments and discomforts. But Ixtepejanos by no means consider drinking to be a bed of roses and are just as ready to talk about bad side effects. The main negative result is the inevitable hangover, or *cruda*, which follows a drinking bout. In addition, aside from the sheer physical discomfort, there is the loss of working time due to incapacitation. Because of this, when a man has a particular job that must be done on the following day or so, he is apt to take special precautions not to get involved in a drinking situation. This often means staying in the fields until he can slip back into his house at night, or perhaps remaining at home all day. Because of the inevitable hangover and incapacitation, there is an ambivalence toward drinking. However, Ixtepejanos regard these undesirable side effects as a form of punishment. But this is not due to guilt, for having overindulged, in the usual Protestant sense. They conceive of it rather as an arbitrary and basically meaningless natural phenomenon that is an unavoidable consequence to be endured if one is to experience the desirable effects of drinking. Informants describe this negative aspect of drinking when asked, but most often express it in metaphors and sayings. For example, "to give one a drink" is sometimes expressed as *pegarle* (to hit him), or as giving him a *castigo* (punishment).

Drinking Patterns

Ixtepeji is an "alcohol culture." Group drinking is an essential part of virtually every occasion where adults, especially men, come together. Ceremonial events such as numerous religious and political fiestas, weddings, and funerals are occasions for hard drinking, lasting perhaps up to three or four days, during which Ixtepejanos may drink themselves into oblivion several times. Men are the main participants in these bouts, and usually stay in groups physically separated from women, who remain in the background, preparing food and tending children. Hard drinking tends to occur sporadically, being determined more by social context than by individual sense of need. Between drinking sessions individuals may drink little and actively avoid drinking. There seems to be little, if any, physiological addiction in that individuals who are relatively regular heavy drinkers display no withdrawal symptoms when sober. "Alcoholism" exists only in the sense that some persons irregularly but frequently drink to the point of unconsciousness. Social and cultural patterns are therefore more important etiological factors then physiological addiction. These data are consistent with other observations of primitive and peasant societies where alcoholism is not necessarily a function of either the concentration or quantity of alcohol consumed (*cf.* Heath 1958:32, Simmons 1960:37).

The alcoholic beverages that Ixtepejanos drink are *mezcal, tepache,* and beer. Mezcal, a distillate of the maguey plant (*Agave spp.*), was formerly prepared in Ixtepeji, but no one has done so for about fifteen years. The mezcal sold in town, although harsher in taste than finer brands, has a lower alcohol content, and Ixtepejanos prefer it for this reason, pointing out that stronger mezcal is more deleterious to health. Relative price is also a factor in their preference for the cruder form.

There are three types of tepache in the state of Oaxaca. The only one that is drunk in Ixtepeji is made from fermented juice of the maguey. In areas of sugar cane and pineapple, a similar beverage is made from these plants also. Virtually all of the tepache consumed in the town is locally prepared, although when the supply of maguey juice is insufficient to meet the needs of a large fiesta, it is bought either in Oaxaca or neighboring towns. Because of the ease of its preparation, tepache can be—and from time to time is—prepared in individual households. However, several persons who have a reputation for doing so produce the greater volume of it. In most cases they are also owners of stores who have a ready means of disposing of large quantities before they spoil.

There are two distinct patterns in which the three alcoholic beverages— beer, tepache, and mezcal—are consumed; we may refer to them as "sipping" and "ritual." Sipping consists of a group of men, usually two to five, sitting together and casually drinking while smoking and chatting. Beer is always drunk in this manner and perhaps half of the tepache. In this context there is little difference from drinking soft drinks. Little attention is paid to the beverage as such, as most of the action and attention focuses on dialogue. In ritual drinking, the beverage per se is central and mediates between a role dyad consisting of a group, represented by an individual acting as a server, and a receiver, as opposed to the members of a loosely constituted group of sippers. In this pattern of interaction, the server approaches the receiver and, while pouring, offers him the drink. The receiver takes the drink, raises it to those present, says *Salud*, those near him respond *Recibe* as he drinks it. There are two basic variations of this fundamental situation; one may be called "formal ritual" and the other "informal ritual." Formal ritual occurs, for example, at a fiesta dinner or an official function in the courthouse. In such situations, the receivers are aligned in a rough order depending on official position or prestige rank. The server with bottle and glass in hand starts at the upper end and serves individuals in turn, with the implicit assumption that all will accept; there are rarely refusals in this pattern. The informal situation is essentially the same with the following variations. The group is not linearly arranged but usually consists of men milling or sitting at random around a room, engaged in side conversations rather than focusing attention on the server–receiver interaction. In this case, the server is usually self-appointed and probably more intoxicated than the others. Periodically, he will take it upon himself to gather up bottle and glass and serve those present, usually following a rough prestige rank order. In this pattern, the receiver usually refuses to accept on the first offer. The server then becomes insistent and presses the glass on him. Thus a sequence of offering— refusal—inducement—acceptance is acted out. There is a strong feeling of obligation to accept, even when the drink is sincerely not wanted, and in almost all instances where the receiver at first refuses, he eventually accepts. If the receiver is resolute in his refusal, he is likely to accept the glass, raise it, mumble a few words to those present, and then hand it to another, saying, "Drink it in my stead." The reasons given for not accepting are either that the receiver has already taken a certain amount or is sick. There is, however, no valid excuse for not drinking. So strong is the pressure to accept that the receiver who does not want to drink will sometimes take the drink but hold the liquid in his mouth, spitting it out when the server has turned his back. This insistence on having all present participate is reflected in a saying, *No se puede escapar a las copas* (One cannot escape the cups).

Attitudes toward the beverage in ritual situations are strikingly different from those in sipping where it is often enjoyed as such and drunk slowly. In contrast, in the formal situations, the beverage is an ordeal a server presses on the receiver, something that he must endure and get over with as quickly as possible. Thus, when the drink has been presented to the receiver, he holds it for a moment with head bowed slightly, as though mentally preparing himself. Then after a few fleeting glances to either side as if to confirm that others are watching, with a look of resolve, a sucking in of air, a slight stiffening of the body, he will mutter a salud or two and abruptly raise the glass to his lips while jerking his head back, throwing the liquid into his mouth. There then follows a shudder of the body and head and a contorted grimace in which he tightly shuts lips and eyes. The sequence is completed by turning the head to one side and letting a large ball of saliva fall from his lips.

As noted above, the drinking pattern of tepache is situationally dependent, being sipped as a soft drink, or drunk ritually. In ritual contexts, although it is served in large cups or water glasses, there is no sipping and it is drunk down rapidly, as is a shot of mezcal, the only difference being that the larger volume takes longer to consume.

One other drinking pattern consists of individuals buying drinks across the counter in stores. There are no cantinas in Ixtepeji. However, several small *tiendas* (stores) are the scene of much drinking. Here, when the receiver is paying for his own drink, the ritual server-receiver interaction does not occur and there are less aspects of ordeal, although, in the case of mezcal, there is the inevitable look of resolve, the fast tossing down of the liquid, and the facial grimace. This is the only situation in which women drink in public, and they usually explain that it is for some medicinal reason.

A common scene is as follows. A small group will be drinking in a store, a home, or perhaps standing on a street corner. Someone will come into sight; if he is an acquaintance of and on good terms with the group, it is almost inevitable that one of them will attract his attention and invite him to drink with them. The invited person will most likely refuse, whereupon the person inviting him will become more insistent and perhaps, if they are in a store, order him a drink. Should the invited person persist in his refusal, he will always leave and have no further intercourse with the group in that setting. Should he accept, however, it is as though a magic door were opened into the group which now permits a degree of familiarity that contrasts with the distance existing before his acceptance. The increase of distance created by a refusal finds expression in derogatory epithets often muttered as the person who has refused the invitation departs. The most frequent explanation for this strong social pressure to have all who are present in a drinking situation participate is that a nondrinking individual is in a position to take advantage of those who are drinking. This is because, as informants say, when drinking "one is more open and less able to defend himself."

Etiological Factors

Various authors have formed hypotheses about inebriety, in so called "primitive" societies, based on correlations with social and psychological variables. Here the Ixtepeji data will be compared with some of these observations, and then a relatively unrecognized motivation to drink will be discussed.

Anxiety and Social Stress. Following Horton's (1943) cross-cultural study many investigators have sought the cause of male insobriety in various types of anxiety. Horton had found that anxieties resulting primarily from financial insecurity correlated with drunkenness. Horton also attempted to demonstrate that "drinking of alcohol tends to be accompanied by the release of sexual and aggressive impulses." He further explained that since these impulses are often punished, a counteranxiety is created such that the "strength of the drinking response tends to vary inversely with the strength of the counteranxiety elicited by painful experiences during and after drinking" (Horton 1943:230).

Other investigators have made criticisms and modifications of Horton's anxiety hypothesis. Before mentioning them, it is worth recalling that there is a fundamentally negative view of living conditions in Ixtepeji. Although there is little concern with actual starvation, there is considerable anxiety about food, health, death, and physical and supernatural aggression, plus the general belief that local conditions are deteriorating. Widespread practice of witchcraft is a particularly insidious major cause of anxiety. The Ixtepeji life style thus supports Horton's first two hypotheses, concerning release of aggressive impulses when drinking, and the correlation of drinking response with the level of anxiety. However, it does not support the third hypothesis, which inversely relates drinking and counteranxiety. Although there is considerable counteranxiety, it is not a significant force in reducing the drinking of the total society, even though it does have some significance in a few individual cases.

Field, after an extensive reexamination of Horton's explanations of the functions of alcohol in primitive societies concluded "that the degree of drunkenness at periodic communal drinking bouts is related to variables indicating a personal (or informal) rather than a corporate (or formal) organization, but is substantially unrelated to the level of anxiety in the society" (Field 1962:72).

Some of the variables Field found correlated with relative sobriety can instructively be compared with the Ixtepeji material:

1. *Corporate kin groups with continuity over time, collective ownership of property, and unified action as a legal individual (Field 1962:72).* In Ixtepeji, kinship is characteristically weakly developed, with the boundaries of the nuclear family as the actual and preferred extent of effective kin ties. There is a strong desire for individual self-sufficiency that runs through the entire society, and accounts for the virtual nonexistence of corporate groups and voluntary associations. Ixtepeji drinking thus is in accord with Field's hypothesis.

Field, on the basis of his correlations, implicitly argues that drinking occurs as a result of poor social integration, viz., in societies that tend toward anomie. There is, however, reason to believe that drinking results not as a negative effect of anomie, but rather functions to counteract it, by augmenting social integration.

Heath (1958) makes this argument for the function of drinking among the individualistically oriented and introverted Camba of Bolivia, and Mangin (1957) stresses the integrative functions of drinking among the Quechua of Peru, as Platt (1955) does for the South African Bantu, and Bunzel (1940) for the Indians of Chichicastenango, Guatemala, and the Madsens (1969) for the Indians of Tecospa, Mexico. We must also note that although drinking is largely disruptive in Ixtepeji, it also oils much social interaction and increases self expression in dancing and music.

2. *Patrilocal residence at marriage.* Patrilocality (living with the family of the groom) is the most common Ixtepeji pattern for the first year or so after marriage. Although Field (1962:72) finds patrilocality positively correlated with relative sobriety, Simmons (1960) argues that, in a Peruvian peasant community similar to Ixtepeji, parental reluctance to relinquish land and authority results in aggression in adult male children, which is released by drinking. This form of child–parent dissension also occurs in the strongly patripotestal Ixtepeji family, in which fathers are often reluctant to confer on sons the economic means necessary for an independent life. Thus, whereas Field finds that absence of drunkenness "appears to be associated with male dominance reflected in patrilocal and perhaps avunculocal residence" (1962:59), the contrary is the case in Ixtepeji.[1]

3. *The last of Field's correlations relevant to Ixtepeji is "a village settlement pattern (rather than nomadism)"* (1962:72). Contrary to Field's generalization, Ixtepeji's fairly dense village demography is contrary to the individualistic orientation of Ixtepeji drinkers and an associated desire of theirs for privacy and secretiveness in personal affairs, which they regard as the best defense against witchcraft and aggression in general. Village life thus not only provides more possibility for aggression because of more intense personal interaction, but also raises the level of social anxiety.

Examination of Ixtepeji social organization and world view in cross-cultural perspective reveals the above cited parallels and differences with other similar societies with much drunkenness. A search for a single or even a few main causes of heavy drinking is doubtlessly futile; multiple and probably variable causes exist in any given society. After prolonged participation in Ixtepeji society I was drawn to conclude that all of the above conditions are probably contributing factors, but that there is also another major motivation not frequently mentioned in the literature on alcoholism.

Drinking as a Means of Transcendence

Life is difficult in Ixtepeji. Chapter 12 discusses certain culturally patterned ways of adjusting to the local environment, which Ixtepejanos perceive as largely negative and lacking many desired qualities. Alcohol is central in one of these

---

[1] Of relevance here is the widespread Mexican taboo of sons drinking in the presence of their fathers. This taboo functions to prevent sons, whose restraints have been lowered by alcohol, from overtly expressing repressed hostility toward fathers, and thus disrupting the patriarchal family.

compensations which we shall consider here. In short, it is the attempt to create temporary ideal environments by symbolically maximizing positively valued conditions. This occurs in certain ritual contexts, especially fiestas. As far as fulfilling this latent function, fiestas are artificially created microcosmic ideal environments. These predominantly male events characteristically begin with a large group of men packing into the sponsor's house to the sound of loud music and fireworks. The house is inevitably too small, thus throwing everyone into physical contact. Room is then made for the municipal band. The noise level of the music and the voices of men shouting to be heard above it become deafening as windows and doors are shut, as though to shut out the outside world and contain the atmosphere within. Ritualized drinking and speech making then begin. The themes of these "orations" vary little from one to another, as they eloquently invert normal existence. They reaffirm how all present are "brothers," are all "sons of the town," or of their *barrio*, and they praise the "glorious" past of the town and its present "honor," "virtue," and "security." As the alcohol begins to take effect, the men draw into closer physical contact, something that normally only young people and women do. Their speech becomes more intimate as they "open up," while at the same time they remain on guard lest someone take offense. And all this takes place amidst mountainous quantities of food—more than is ever eaten—as if to affirm that here, at least, there will be no hunger.

The personality of the participants and the content of speech at fiestas contrasts dramatically with those of everyday life. One informant expressed his reaction to alcohol in such a setting thus: "After a few cups I feel very happy and gay and talk better; I feel stronger and at times almost invincible." The Mexican poet Octavio Paz has also expressed this alteration of the everyday world; "The fiesta is something more than a date or an anniversary. It does not celebrate, but reproduces an event: it splits open normal time so that, for the space of a few short immeasurable hours, the eternal present reinstates itself. The fiesta becomes creator of time. Repetition becomes conception. Time is born. The age of gold returns" (Paz 1959:189; my translation).

The casual observer is prone to be overly concerned with the end result of fiesta drinking, that is, the unconscious torpor of *sangre de cuche*, which is seen as an "escape" from the realities of life. Such an explanation of motivation to drink is contrary to reasons given by the people themselves, who are quick to emphasize that this phase of the drinking cycle is undesirable, especially the inevitable *cruda*, which is an unavoidable consequence one must suffer to experience the desired effects of drinking. These two contrary results of drinking thus produce a strong ambivalence toward alcohol.

Looked at in the above light, drinking is much more than an escape from life into a drunken stupor; it is instead a vehicle to transcend the mundane daily world. Escape is achieved by anesthesia, but at the fiesta the senses are bombarded with stimuli—physical, auditory, and emotional—all of which serve to intensify the experience and affirm the individual's existence. This is a theme pervading Mexican culture, manifested in an affinity for excitement, loud noise, bright colors, and emotionally stirring experiences, all of which are epitomized in the fiesta. Often when walking through a desolate countryside, I have been startled by adult companions rending the silence with a spontaneous *grita* (shout), or by firing off a few gun shots, which are intended to *quitar la tristeza* (remove the sadness).

The desire to intensify experience in the present is consistent with temporal concepts, in Ixtepeji, which, as we have seen, are predominantly oriented to the present and the past. As indicated above, the future is seen as uncertain, and tending to bring worse conditions. One therefore attempts to exploit present conditions and resources to the fullest, while opportunity exists. As we have seen there are few valuable resources thought to exist in the local environment, which can be maximized. But one resource over which the individual has some control and which he can augment is personal experience, especially emotionally moving experience, best typified in the fiesta. Alcohol is the main agent necessary for this transformation.

Nietzsche (1872) described this "Dionysian" desire to transcend regular existence, through excess, in his analysis of Greek tragedy; Ruth Benedict later took up this notion and characterized the cultures of American Indians of the Northwest Coast and the Great Plains as Dionysian cultures. This is also an apt characterization of Ixtepejanos at fiestas. The Dionysian seeks

> 'the annihilation of the ordinary bounds and limits of existence'; he seeks to attain in his most valued moments escape from the boundaries imposed upon him by his five senses, to break through into another order of experience. The desire of the Dionysian, in personal experience or in ritual, is to press through it toward a certain psychological state, to achieve excess. The closest analogy to the emotions he seeks is drunkenness, and he values the illuminations of frenzy (Benedict 1959:79).

There is much psychological distance between individuals in Ixtepeji. Alcohol serves to dissolve this individualism. But more than this, it coalesces individuals into a community momentarily dedicated to transforming perceived reality from a world of loneliness, suffering, and deprivation, into one of brotherhood, happiness, and general well-being.

Ambivalence toward Drinking

The act of communal drinking has a built-in double bind in which the process of getting drunk induces two contrary states of being. One is the desired exhilaration described above; the second is a coincidental and negatively valued condition. As previously indicated, the most common explicit reason for drinking is to produce "happiness" and "excitement," and to remove "sadness." But there is a striking difference in the stated reasons and the thematic content of the conversation occurring in drinking situations. The main themes constantly repeated are unity, security, and absence of violence, with an emphasis on friendship, brotherhood, and common background and membership. As in similar cases where a given condition is constantly reiterated, there is reason to suspect the latent existence of its opposite. In this case, these speech forms mask latent hostile emotions that threaten to erupt in violence and to disintegrate a precarious group solidarity. This is the double bind that communal drinking involves, for the process of getting drunk and achieving the desired results—absence of ennui and melancholy—also lowers the restraining forces that contain unexpressed hostility, which may explode when *sangre de chango* turns into *sangre de león.* It is as though all the emphasis on friendship, security, and unity is to serve as a constant reminder that the state of sangre de león is dangerous, and all precaution is necessary to pass through it to the stuporous safety of *sangre de cuche.*

The extent of this expressed concern with restraint of violence and a complementary affirmation of friendship, security, and confidence that occurs in drinking situations cannot be overemphasized. An example will demonstrate how it operates in a typical setting: One Sunday Patricio Mejía was in his house drinking and talking with two of his compadres who had come to town for a baptism. About an hour before the food was served one of the men was almost too drunk to sit in his chair. Patricio and the other men were still fairly sober and drinking more slowly. They were drinking beer, mezcal, and tepache. Beers were being individually served and sipped; tepache was being served to all and drunk by all simultaneously, and mezcal was served by the formal ritual system. As the drunk man started falling out of his chair, the others suggested that he lie down to rest. He refused and exerted all his energy to stay in the chair. In trying to persuade him to lie down, Patricio repeatedly used phrases such as, "with all confidence," "in safety," "have no worry," "you are among friends," "you are in your own house," etc., which in their literal sense emphasize the idea of safety and lack of danger in going to sleep in Patricio's house. Later he explained several times how all were together because it was Sunday, the day to rest after a week of hard work, and how all were drinking and talking in such a peaceful manner. He dwelt frequently on how all were in his house with confidence, friendship, and safety, since there would be no trouble of any kind—phrases replicating the same themes he used to persuade his compadre to lie down. Again, these continuously repeated assurances suggest that it is advisable to consider the existence of the opposite. Patricio seemed to be implicitly saying, that this was really a tense and precarious situation because everyone was drinking; one man was already drunk and getting belligerent, and all the potential violence that was smoldering in each man could come boiling out if precautions were not taken to keep it bottled in.

This concern with restraint of violence and aggression in drinking situations stems from the realization that alcohol is involved in almost all common acts of violence, such as fisticuffs, wife beatings, and physical abuse of children, as well as more serious ones.

Case Histories

Although it is difficult to quantify such material, it appears that most acts of violence while intoxicated are done by men between the ages of about thirty-five and fifty. From such general observations and comparisons of life histories, it is possible to speak of an alcoholic syndrome that develops in varying degrees in the life cycle of some men. The most notable feature of this syndrome is the onset, in middle age, of an increase in overt expression of suppressed hostility under the influence of alcohol. Another symptom is a dramatic and extreme transformation in personality that individuals undergo when drunk. Someone who when sober is the epitome of a polite, congenial, and sympathetic man becomes, after a few drinks, a belligerent, truculent, and overbearing *macho* who regards the slightest remark about his character or reluctance to comply with his wishes as a personal insult and cause for physical retaliation.

The case history of Abelardo Juárez, age forty-five, illustrates the development of this syndrome. Abelardo began to seek me out when he heard that I had an interest in drinking and curing. His expressed reason for doing so was to find out if I had any special knowledge or means to aid him with his "sickness," since local healers had failed to cure him. When sober, Abelardo is one of the kindest and most considerate people in Ixtepeji. With the exception of his behavior when drunk, relatives and friends describe him as a very good man and especially as an ideal father. He has nine children, five of whom are through school, and everyone is quick to point out that although Abelardo is poorer than most men of the town, he has spared no effort to maintain his family. In addition to taking care of their subsistence needs, he has worked hard to earn money as a muleteer. But the problem is that with mezcal Mr. Hyde appears.

Abelardo himself expresses his problem well: "I can't drink much now. Up until I was thirty-seven I could drink night and day and never forget anything that happened. But now after two shots I forget everything. And when I am like this, I try to hit and mistreat any person that may be around. Before, I was fortunate because after I got drunk to a certain point, I would just fall down and go to sleep, but now I have the disadvantage of not falling as before; now I just stay on my feet and keep drinking and causing trouble." He is quick to stress what a good person he is when sober and how he dislikes violence and trouble. He is especially distressed by the way in which he mistreats his wife and children when drunk, since on numerous occasions he has physically injured them. As his aunt says, "After a few swallows he wants to kill." The most reasonable explanation that he can conceive of, which is in accord with common folk beliefs, is as follows:

> When I first started forgetting and having these problems, I had a hired man who was helping me. He lived with a bad woman. One time before All Souls' Day we invited them to our house. She began to scold him a great deal, and when I asked her why, she started on me, and later she bewitched me with black magic and in this way dominated me. When I woke up, I was stretched out on a mat surrounded by my family who thought I was dying. The woman gave it to me, she gave me this disease. Later she told me that she did it in a moment when she forgot God. It all started with this."

But other factors are involved. As his aunt also points out, there are people who are jealous of Abelardo because he has so many well-behaved and well-dressed children, and that therefore envy may have motivated them to attack him by witchcraft.

In drinking problems such as Abelardo's, nearly all attention focuses on causes and cures centering on notions of witchcraft and other folk beliefs. There is almost no concern with associated social factors such as the many institutionalized and semi-institutionalized patterns that compel individuals to drink, operating in formal drinking situations typified by the saying, "You can't escape the cups," and also in informal settings that are even more pervasive and harder to escape by someone who does not wish to drink. In Abelardo's case, it is primarily these informal drinking situations that cause him the most trouble. The following incidents illustrate the extent of this problem: On several occasions when he arranged to come and talk in my house, he would do so only on the condition that I come across town to meet him at his house and accompany him back to mine. The reason for this arrangement was that these were days when he knew there would be many men about drinking in places he would have to pass and into which they would invite him. The pressures to join into such situations and the implications of refusal were such that he did not wish to take the risks involved. Such situations created for him the dilemma that, on the one hand, he had to suffer the recriminations and ill will of those he might refuse to drink with, and on the other, if he did begin drinking, he ran the risk of blacking out and becoming violent, not to mention the discomfort of a bad hangover. The best way to avoid the problem was to stay close to home or go to the fields. His reasoning for having me come to get him was that I, as an outsider, could more graciously refuse the inevitable invitations, and also excuse him by explaining that he had an obligation to me.

A similar case history is that of Cristobal, age forty-five. Cristobal lives with his second wife and her young daughter and three of his children, ages four to fourteen. When sober, Cristobal is as congenial as Abelardo. He is ostensibly well esteemed by most people, and in 1966–1967 held a major town office, an indication of his status in the community. But when drunk, Cristobal, like Abelardo, becomes another man with whom no one wishes to reckon. Frequent drinking bouts take place in his house, of which the members of his family are the main victims. Cristobal's drunken behavior is typically that which he tries with so much effort to prevent in drinking situations. In Cristobal's case, the fact that he is a witch intensifies the problem. Because of this additional factor he is considered particularly dangerous when he gets out of hand.

Drinking and Religious Conversion

A problem of increasing concern for Ixtepejanos is a growing number of Protestant converts in the town and in the Sierra Juárez in general. The predominant Protestant denomination is the Seventh Day Adventists, members of which are referred to as *sabadistas* because they observe the Sabbath on Saturday. Sabadistas have been present in the Sierra in significant numbers for about twenty years, during which time the greater Catholic population has quietly but strongly opposed them. Because of this opposition, which usually takes the form of economic sanctions, gossip, and ostracism, it is almost impossible for sabadistas to live in Ixtepeji. Most of them are now scattered on small ranches in the mountains. Only in the nearby settlements of Tierra Colorada and El Punto are they numerous enough to hold their own, and in Tierra Colorada they even elect some officials.

Direct questions about the basis of the opposition against the sabadistas elicit stereotyped explanations such as: They are enemies of God; They are agents of the Devil; They say the priests are lying; They are against the Church; and so forth. But although the usual objections to the sabadistas and Protestants in general are phrased in religious terms, the real motivation for wishing to suppress them is that, upon conversion, people stop drinking, and therefore stop participating in the various community and individually sponsored fiestas. A significant number of local nonparticipants is thus viewed as a direct threat to the most anticipated events of the otherwise monotonous yearly cycle. Nearby Ixtlán and Yotao now are said to have poor fiestas because they are "divided by religion."

Given that there are strong social sanctions against the sabadistas, the question arises as to why they should continue their practices and why they should continue to gain converts. Some answers can be found by examining a case history. Juan Yescas, fifty-nine, is the son-in-law of Bernardino Salcido, the first convert in town. Bernardino first converted his daughter who in turn, with Bernardino, converted Juan. Juan's wife and their grown children have been living in Oaxaca City for several years, since life in Ixtepeji became too difficult for them. Juan, however, spends most of the year in the town because he must care for his land. When he is not working in his fields or away at weekly sabadista meetings, he lives like a hermit in his house, which is in the center of town.

As is often the case, Juan's position in the town is the reverse of what he says. Almost his first words to me were to the effect that no one molested him, that because he has terminated his civic duties and pays his taxes, people therefore leave him in peace. Such statements are belied by a large permanent barricade at the entrance to his patio and the fact that he never goes on the streets of town, but instead takes paths that lead directly to the fields.

In later conversations, a more realistic picture of his position in town came out. As he says, "I have much Catholic family here, but they don't have anything to do with me because I am an evangelist. Before I used to talk with them a lot, but now they don't understand me." Referring to the town in general, he says, "I don't have anything to do with them, nor they with me. They don't want any evangelists here." As he explains, he is essentially a *persona non grata* in the eyes of the townspeople. "They call me *El Protestante* because I don't join with them. Because of this the town officers will not listen to me here." Other informants verify this, explaining how Juan would be completely ignored if he were to bring a matter to the court. Juan himself pretends to be aloof from all this by saying that no one here would do him any great damage since they all know that he would take a complaint to higher authorities. Juan's only friend in town is a young man, Rogelio Ortiz, a cousin of his wife. Rogelio stops by to visit with Juan occasionally, but even he is likely to taunt Juan by offering him cigarettes, which he knows he will refuse, or by inviting him for a drink.

A clue as to why Juan maintains his religion is suggested from his lengthy talk about it. Surprisingly little of his discussion is of a religious nature. Instead, the main points that he emphasizes are the sins of those who have not converted and the way that they mistreat him. When talking about the "sins" of his Catholic neighbors, he continually returns to one point, namely that they all drink alcohol, and drink to excess.

This is enough to suggest the hypothesis that drinking is the pivotal point in the Catholic–Protestant opposition, the question of fiesta participation being one aspect of it. In brief, the hypothesis can be stated as follows: The strong social coercions to drink pose a painful dilemma to many men. On one hand they do not wish to suffer the sanctions and suspicion that result from not drinking, but on the other, drinking often becomes an ordeal that they would like to avoid. It is an ordeal first in the very real physical discomfort, often an agony, that is the usual consequence of a drinking session. Here there is of course marked individual variations, but of 23 known converts, 20 are middle-aged men who have histories of hard drinking. Drinking for these men is perhaps even more of a mental, rather than a physical, ordeal because of the culturally determined psychological responses that include severe delerium tremens, the hallucinatory content of which is suggested by the most unpleasant aspects of folk belief and folklore. There is also in such individuals a strong moral self-reprehension resulting from acts of violence and meanness performed when alcohol releases suppressed hostilities and aggressive impulses. In addition, drunken behavior is a cause for men's concern about their own physical and legal safety. And finally there is an economic factor resulting from the money spent on drinking, plus the incapacitation to work. All of these are reasons for "wanting out" of the drinking complex, but for any one individual this is an almost impossible problem since drinking is so firmly embedded in the culture. It is comparable to an alcoholic wanting to sober up while living with 500 other alcoholics. In psychiatric terms it could be said that the support therapy is not good. It is here that religious conversion becomes important. By becoming a member of a sect that specifically forbids drinking or even participation in events where drinking occurs, the individual wishing to get out of the drinking pattern has a ready-made alternate mode of behavior that he can assume, backed up by an alternate supernatural sanction system, and, even more importantly, by a group of sympathetic people who are grappling with the same problems. Again, as mentioned above, almost all cases of male converts are in fact middle-aged men who have had severe drinking problems and a strongly developed aversion to drinking. Similarly, Catholics, when pointing out the undesirable results of drinking, often mention that abstinence is a good feature of the sabadista religion.

Juan Yescas is a typical example of a man who, before his conversion, had a drinking problem, which he himself explains as one of the main reasons for converting. In all his talk of his relation to non-Protestants, he points out that they drink and he does not and that this is a reason why he cannot walk through the streets of the town or associate with other men. "They drink because they say it is a remedy, but it isn't; it injures one and does much damage." On the other side, gossip about Juan tells what an odd creature he is, living alone and not drinking, "like a woman." But that he has not achieved complete immunity is suggested by tales of how several times during *tequio* the men forced him to drink and that, once he got started, he did not stop until he fell down in the street.

Some years ago an event involving drinking and religious difference disrupted the town. At this time, the *primer regidor* was a sabadista who did not drink. However, in such a case the custom is that "one must adapt to and obey the town's wishes." This man avoided the problem by being absent as much as possible. But it happened that the municipal president had to leave town for personal reasons. This left the regidor as representative of the town for six months, during which time the town fiesta was to occur. During all of the preliminary functions of the fiesta he consistently refused to drink. Finally public reaction got so strong that some of the sponsors of the fiesta threatened to disband and thus cancel it. This was an inconceivable disaster; however, they would have been able to do it in such a manner that all the blame would have fallen on the regidor. He was thus placed in an impossible situation and soon gave in. It is said that after a few cups of mezcal and tepache, he could not stop and got very drunk. Shortly thereafter he renounced his religion and resumed drinking.

Summary

The material presented in this chapter draws several conclusions. First, there is a complex set of social, psychological, and environmental conditions involved in the etiology of alcoholism or drunkenness in Ixtepeji. I have suggested that, of these, the main motivation to drink is to intensify emotional experience as a means of momentarily transcending a negatively perceived social and geographic environment. Ixtepejanos do not, therefore, drink to "escape" into stupor, which is an undesirable final outcome of drinking. Second, the dynamics of occasional individuals' disaffiliation from the drinking pattern is best seen as a gain–loss decision-making process in which the traumatic effects of drinking are weighed against the negative social sanctions that accompany abstinence. Finally, conversion to a religious sect that requires abstinence provides support, which in part offsets the negative sanctions; this type of religious conversion is therefore of important therapeutic value.

11

La Llorona:
Symbol of Family
and Interpersonal Relations

IN PREVIOUS CHAPTERS we have looked at single aspects of world view and
society in Ixtepeji. This chapter now integrates these propositions and demonstrates more fully the relationship between them and social interaction. As a
way of doing this the unconscious logic of a folktale is analyzed so that we can
see how it is a mirror of daily social life.

One of the most widespread Mexican folktale themes is about *La Llorona,*
the Weeping Woman, a nocturnal being who is heard crying for her lost children.
The antiquity of the story cannot be determined but it is evident from early Colonial texts that the theme is pre-Hispanic in the central highlands. It apparently
existed in two forms: La Llorona crying for her children and La Llorona as a
seducer of men. The most common contemporary version is a fusion of these two
prototypes; Horcasitas and Butterworth have reconstructed it as follows:

> La Llorona was an Indian woman who had several illegitimate children. When
> her lover rejected her she went out of her mind and drowned her children in a
> river. After her death she was compelled to search for them every night. Nowadays
> she appears as a beautiful woman. She has long hair and is dressed in white.
> Men are attracted to her, follow her, and she leads them away to dangerous places.
> Often they are found dead (Horcasitas and Butterworth 1963:221–222).

With a few minor variations this type is a good composite of La Llorona
tales in Ixtepeji. Whether the Llorona legend existed in pre-Hispanic Oaxaca or
was borrowed from other regions after the Conquest is uncertain. However, a variant of La Llorona occurs in Ixtepeji bearing the name *Matlaziwa.* Matlaziwa is a
spirit-being who is similar enough to La Llorona so that informants tend to equate
them. In Ixtepeji, La Llorona and Matlaziwa are significant beings. Everyone knows
of them and many people report having heard, seen, and had direct encounters
with them. Analysis of La Llorona and Matlaziwa tales yields the following predominant themes:

1. *Aire.* The theme of *aire* is perhaps the most obvious. In an earlier chapter we saw how the concept of aire, which is important in Spanish–American folk beliefs about disease etiology, serves to symbolize the perceived social and geographic environment, which Ixtepejanos view as inherently hostile and constantly menacing the individual. In Ixtepeji, man walks through the social world, the natural landscape, and the realm of the supernatural, constantly on guard against threatening people, spirits, and objects. They are motivated mainly by *muina*, an internalized anger, resulting mainly from envy, which causes people and spirits to want to harm others. Their main mode of attack is to deceive their victim so that he will be off guard and let his defenses down. In many instances, La Llorona and Matlaziwa are directly equated with aire, and in others they are attributed aire-like qualities. La Llorona "goes flying through the air" and "She goes about like the air. She lost her soul because of her evil deeds; God does not receive such people, he leaves them in the free air." In other words, the air is filled with malevolent souls, which are wandering about in agony and are therefore dangerous. "God does not allow the people to see her," that is, she is invisible as the air.

2. *Deception and Treachery.* La Llorona is invisible, however, only until she reveals herself to her victim, which she does only to deceive him. She never appears as what she is, but rather as a beautiful woman who entices him with her charms, or as a person he should be able to trust such as his wife or *novia* (sweetheart). In the Matlaziwa stories, the apparition may appear as a friend or merely some normal person. Once she has performed her deceit (*engaño*) and gained the confidence of her unsuspecting victim, she works her treachery by doing him bodily injury. The places and methods she chooses are, as we shall see, also significant.

3. *Abandonment, Suffering, and Fatalism.* Although the term *abandonado*, which is common in song and poetry, is not frequently used in the La Llorona accounts, the tales usually begin with La Llorona as a mother who abandons or kills her children. Since the tales are about her and not the children, her fate resulting from this act is the subject of the rest of the tale. From this point on she is a person destined to an eternity of suffering, which is a punishment from God for her evil deed. In contrast to European themes of sin and punishment, there is no concern with redemption or atonement here. On the contrary, her punishment is absolute and irrevocable; rather than being purified or redeemed, she becomes the embodiment of insidious characteristics that in turn move her to harm others.

Many informants emphasize that it is the mother's betrayal, her treachery, that sets the morbid drama in motion. To appreciate the meaning of this motif, it is necessary to recall something of child training, especially the mother–child relationship, where it is the child's mother who first betrays him; his first lessons in deceit and deception (*engaño*) are learned at her breast. In Chapter 6 we saw that a common method of controlling children is to lie to them, either by promising them some reward with no intention of fulfilling it, or, more frequently, by threatening them with some frightening punishment, again with no intent of actually carrying it out. This latter practice usually takes the form of threatening to abandon the child (to put it out of the house at night where wild animals or La Llorona can get it, or by leaving it along the road, or by selling it to a stranger). Also, mothers often tell children that if they do not behave, wild animals will come in the night and devour them.

Looked at in this light, the La Llorona tale becomes mythic. What we have are the fragments of a creation myth. It may be seen as a creation myth because it does two things: First, it relates important experiences, perhaps the most important in the psychogenesis of the individual, that is, betrayal by the mother. Whereas in *Oedipus Rex*, Oedipus' fate is determined by the triadic relationship of himself, Laius, and Jocasta, the fate of the Ixtepejano is bound up in the relationship between himself, the absent father, and La Llorona.[1] Second, since in myth the individual is a microcosmic replication of the world view, the legend is also a statement about the world, especially the world of interpersonal relations. In the tale, the child, now appearing as a man, is subject to the same basic *engaño* and omnipresent malevolent forces that he was at the mercy of in the arms of his omnipotent mother. I speak of "forces" because there is also in the myth an explanation of motivation in interpersonal relations as having some force, some concept of energy or drive that vitalizes it and results in action. To reveal this image of human motivation, which not only sets the events of the legend in motion but is also the source of its fateful and tragic nature, let us go back to the beginning.

As in the above prototype and in Ixtepejian texts, La Llorona herself, was the first victim who was betrayed and abandoned; for this she cries "because she can't obtain her own tranquillity." It is this original misfortune of hers compounded by her eternal punishment, which explains her malevolence in terms of a basic tenet of Ixtepejian folk psychology: "A person who is deprived of something wishes to injure and deprive others who are more fortunate." In other words, she, La Llorona, was abandoned by her husband, which caused her great sorrow and *muina*, causing her in turn to kill her babies. Because of this double loss of husband and children, she now envies people more fortunate than herself. For this reason, "she causes married couples to fight" and lose their tranquillity also. Again her method of operation is to deceive or trick, by lies or illusion, her unwary victim who is especially vulnerable when intoxicated and unable to "defend himself." This common verbal usage is expressive of concepts of a self-defending individual vis-a-vis threatening entities. It correlates in the tales with nakedness (in many accounts, La Llorona leaves her victims naked), a theme which often appears in Ixtepejano's dreams in connection with "defenselessness."

This interpretation of La Llorona's behavior is in accord with the folk beliefs mentioned earlier. In some of the examples, however, there is an apparent inconsistency. According to the logic of both the propositions and the folk beliefs, La Llorona should be attacking other women, especially mothers, who have men. She does do this, but most of her victims are men, especially *parranderos*, or men who are carousing about town at night, which carries the connotation that they are carrying on with women—other women—and that they are neglecting their wives and children.

Obviously, attacking other women's men is a way of attacking those women, but a new motivational force, *venganza* (revenge), appears. The *muina* that the wife has from the husband's betrayal and abandonment generalizes to all members of his species; all men whom, by their actions, she identifies with her husband become subject to the controlled, directed release of her suppressed wrath. To

---

[1] Fischer (1963:246) argues that nuclear family symbolism affords the best means to understand the most important meaning of tales and the emotional responses to them.

further understand the underlying logic for La Llorona's choice of *parranderos* as victims, the reader should understand the quality of male–female relations in Ixtepeji. The predatory male, or *macho* (from the woman's point of view), here appears in the legend almost as an archetype. But now, again, from the woman's point of view the time has come for his just reward, which she is fated to mete out to him.[2] I use the term "fated" intentionally, because it is one of the most recurrent characteristics attributed to La Llorona, and because it is the key to understanding the motivation of the personages involved. Let us first consider these personages in their simplest structural relationship, which is male to female. Thus reduced, we can recount the events of the legend in the following sequence:

1. Man abandons woman
2. Mother drowns male child
3. God punishes mother
4. Woman harms man (who is abandoning females)

When we arrive at the fourth step in the sequence, we are in effect again at the beginning. In its internal logic the legend is circular such that event (1) is the cause of event (2), which causes event (3), which causes event (4); the conditions in which (4) occurs, males abandoning women, is equivalent to what happens in (1). In other words, the "system" is self-perpetuating; as an implicit folk model of the antagonistic aspects of male–female relations, it depicts a system in which the actions of the actors are predetermined by the nature of the system itself. The folk model says there is no alternative; a person who is hurt will have muina and desire for revenge, which will compel him to hurt the one who hurt him first. What I speak of as being "compelled" translates in the folk system as being *destinado*, that is, being fated. This is why the concept of fate is the key to understanding the Ixtepeji model of the human motivation expressed in the legend. Besides fateful, I also characterized the legend as tragic, and I meant tragic in the mythical sense also. For, as shown above, the ultimate tragedy derives from the belief that human motivation is at bottom energized and set in motion by that very negative quality, *muina*.

Perhaps at this point the reader has doubts about the circularity of the four stage sequence of the legend and is asking, why should the male in event (1) abandon and so injure his woman as a result of (4), since he is not the same male as the one she attacks in (4); what explains this action of his that starts the tragedy? To answer this, we must not impose our own brand of rational logic onto the legend, but look for meaning in terms of its own logic or symbols. To do this,

---

[2] Women in Ixtepeji are for the most part the passive objects of overt male aggression and sexuality. At least in folklore, however, women retaliate against and control husbands, especially unfaithful ones, by poisoning their food with a preparation containing *Datura meteloides* (*toloache*), which reduces men to a semistupified state described as childlike. Some women know the recipe for this potion, which is associated with the quasi-matriarchal Tehuanas of Tehuantepec, in Southern Oaxaca. Since men are dependent on women for food preparation, this is one area where wives exert control over husbands. In accord with the La Llorona theme, this method is also deceptive, and performed on a victim who is supposedly secure.

let us consider the male characters in the legend, since it is the equivalence of the males of (1) and (4) that seems to be the problem. That (1) and (4) are equivalent is revealed by first comparing male (4) with the child of event (2), the male child the mother drowns. (In the field notes of La Llorona accounts, "children" and "babies" are recorded variously as *hijos, niños,* or *nenes,* all of which in Spanish may refer to males exclusively, or to males and females. In no instance is there a specifically feminine usage.) The male in (4) and the male child in (2) have several features in common. First, La Llorona throws the baby into a well or a river, and similarly she usually shoves the man into a canyon or river. Secondly, the man is sometimes said to be naked, which may be taken as a symbol of being defenseless and childlike. Also the man is usually drunk, which again lowers his ability to defend himself by reducing him to a childlike state. Seen in this way, the males of (2) and (4) are the victims of the dominant female, while in (1) and (3) the woman is the victim of dominant males. We may diagram this as follows, with arrows indicating the direction of the negative actions—*muina,* aggression, and punishment.

$$
\begin{array}{l}
1. \text{ dom. M} \rightarrow \text{def. F} \\
2. \text{ def. M} \leftarrow \text{dom. F} \\
3. \text{ dom. M} \rightarrow \text{def. F} \\
4. \text{ def. M} \leftarrow \text{dom. F}
\end{array}
$$

(dom. = dominant, def. = defenseless, M = male, F = female)

The underlying symmetry is revealed in this reduced structural form, which solves the problem of the equivalence of males (1) and (4). No such problem existed for the female since the tales explicitly maintain her identity as the same individual. But, it is not as an individual that she is significant, but rather as a concatenation of roles: wife, mother, victim of fate, and deceiving seductress. In like manner each of the male elements, which in each stage of the sequence are complementary to the female, may be taken as aspects of the basic male personality which, as with roles, are situationally dependent. Thus the circular relation of the aggressive act, muina, and aggressive act closes, for the victim of La Llorona is really, within the logic of the system, the same dominant male who, because of his own muina and desire for revenge, betrayed his wife in the beginning. Thus we can represent the tale in one final reduced form as follows.

Aggression   Muina

I have described this sequence in a mythic time where linear time is non-existent, and where past, present, and future are equivalent. But insofar as the actual narrative of the tale must be told in progressive time, it is interesting that it begins with betrayal by the male. Is this an indication that it is more a man's world than a woman's?

What the above analysis demonstrates is that this seemingly simple folktale is an elegant and economical representation of the underlying, covert concept of family and interpersonal relations, especially male–female relations. The tale expresses not only the quality of relationships, but also projects a concept of motivation, which is at the same time a statement of human nature.[3]

If the reader has followed the above arguments dealing with muina, envy, and the release of aggression, he is perhaps not yet completely satisfied that the previously mentioned apparent inconsistency is resolved. That is, why are La Llorona's immediate victims almost exclusively men? According to folk belief she should attack married women with children, which she of course does when she attacks men who presumably are married. Could this pattern be explained by the La Llorona tale fulfilling another function in addition to symbolizing interpersonal relations? I suggest that it does. So far we have considered only two possible symbolic functions of the tale, namely the cognitive (existential) and the evaluative— that is, statements about "what is" and "what we would like to be," respectively. A third type, a directive function, or statements about "what should or ought to be," seems to be latent in the content of La Llorona tales (*cf.* Kluckhohn and Strodtbeck 1961:4–5). Thus, while cognitive elements are evident, La Llorona's actions are not entirely consistent with folk ideas of muina and human nature when she attacks primarily men. But, if La Llorona tales are expressing directive propositions, that is, moral propositions, then her behavior is consistent. Consider whom she attacks: either men who are out and about at night, the assumption being that anyone who is out at night is up to no good, or men who are not only out at night, but who are drinking and therefore behaving in the undesirable ways associated with drinking.

To attempt to identify the main symbolic function of La Llorona, that is whether she is most expressive of cognitive, evaluative, or directive propositions, is futile and irrelevant. Along this line Fischer says, "Collectors need not apologize for these apparent contradictions in their texts, since it is those social roles and actions about which people feel most confused which are most likely to become symbolized in myths and tales" (1963:247). What is important to realize is that this seemingly simple tale in fact expresses multiple covert values and perceptions with great symbolic economy.[4]

---

[3] This function of the tale is in accord with the "culture and personality" approach to folklore, which regards it as offering the anthropologist insight into basic personality. "Presumably, folktales also serve a cognitive function for members of the society in educating them about the nature of the local model personality in which all participate . . ." (Fischer 1963: 256–257).

[4] In regard to the type of analysis presented here Mering has said, "Existential values as revealed in mythology arise out of insights into actions taken in their significance for life; and they establish themselves in the culture when the insights can be widely shared" (Mering 1961:75).

12

Adjusting to a Hostile Environment

THE VIEW of life in Ixtepeji is harsh. In it emnity often outweighs friendship, and suffering is commonplace, while happiness is rare. We have seen how in the Ixtepeji view of the world the environment is filled with hostile forces that constantly threaten the individual who attempts to defend himself more by an ability to endure adversity than an attempt to overcome it. The main existential attributes that the Ixtepejano perceives in himself and his local sociogeographical environment are as follows: There is the belief that the weather is becoming more erratic. The land, the basis of life itself, is overworked and becoming less productive. This is a rational conclusion based on observations of decreased crops, soil erosion, deforestation, and population increase. This decline in natural resources is a cause of poverty for which there is no foreseeable solution. The individual sees himself as abandoned to this existence because he is destined to be ineffective before superior, incomprehensible powers. He thinks of himself as poorly equipped to defend himself against these powers because he is ignorant, weak, and alone. The most he can do is struggle on in the face of pain, evil, and sadness. Many affective and cognitive attributes of this negative world are connoted or denoted by often used Spanish terms, words which Bohannan refers to as "key terms" (1963:11–12). Some of these terms, which we looked at earlier, are *engaño, desconfianza, ilusión*, and *soledad*.

Defensive Strategies

Against this view of self and of the local environment is an idealized vision of another world glimpsed in magazines, movies, on trips to the city, or while working as *braceros* in the United States. This other world is one of unlimited wealth and power, one where life is secure and happy, but one that is also forever unattainable.

Perceptions and values of self and the local environment are ones on which

Ixtepejanos operate. The second set, which they attribute to the idealized other, are ones on which they *would like* to operate, but cannot since they are not attributed to self and the local environment. This situation poses an unusual theoretical consideration. Most theories of behavior assume that action is directed toward the maximization of desired entities and conditions. But in Ixtepeji the desired is defined by the world view as unobtainable. Understanding of Ixtepeji psychology, therefore, depends on understanding how man adjusts to a world defined as relatively void of everything desired and filled with all that is negative and threatening. In other words, individuals must make some compensation for such a conception of themselves and their world if life is to be bearable. The widespread use of deception is one way of protecting oneself from perceived dangers (Chapter 7). There are also four other compensatory mechanisms, here called "defensive strategies," which aid adjustment[1] to this surfeit of the negative. ("Defensive strategy" as used here is comparable to the Freudian concept of "defense mechanism," but this new term is used since only one of the mechanisms discussed is a traditional Freudian one.) The four defensive strategies are: 1) repression of desire for the positively valued aspects of life and of conscious awareness of the existing negative ones; 2) the attempt, in special ritual situations, to artificially create an ideal environment; 3) disparagement of self and of referent groups; 4) an individualistic orientation in interpersonal relations and in one's self image. Let us look at these four different ways of coming to terms with the perceived self and the life situation:

1. *Repression.* This term refers to, "The unconscious rejection of perceptions and ideas because of their painful or disagreeable content. The repressed material is submerged into the subconscious but remains dynamic" (Sadler 1953:1141). The perceptions and ideas that the Ixtepejano represses are the disagreeable ones that he identifies with. Repressing them into the subconscious lessens conscious perception of the harshness of the immediate life situation and makes it more bearable. This is not to say that repression of the negative values and perceptions eliminates them or makes them inoperative, but merely that it makes them covert, for they manifest themselves in expressive behavior such as speech forms, dreams, songs, poetry, and folklore (*cf.* Chapters 5 and 11).

This repression is not to be confused with the suppression of hostile emotions (Chapter 7). Repression is an unconscious act, whereas suppression is an intentional inhibition of emotion so as to present the appearance that one is in an emotional state other than the one he is actually in. Suppression therefore also serves a similar defensive function.

2. *Symbolic creation of an ideal environment.* Repression as a compensation to offset perception of the real world as undesirable is consistent with an attempt to create ideal environments by intentional maximization of positively valued conditions. This occurs in ritual contexts, especially fiestas. In fulfilling this latent function, fiestas are artificially created microcosmic ideal environments,

---

[1] "Adjustment" is used here rather than "adaptation" because although both adjustment and adaptation reduce stress, adaptation implies a desirable solution, whereas adjustment is not necessarily desirable. For example, suicide or alcoholism may be adjustive, but not adaptive.

which were described earlier in relation to drinking patterns. Manipulation of symbols in these activities is comparable to Freudian wish-fulfillment in dreaming.

The symbols and symbolic behavior invoked at town meetings are similar to those in fiestas. The pattern of voting in these *asambleas* is typical of group decision-making in general, except that hand or voice votes are taken. The significant point is that no vote is ever taken until there is an unspoken understanding about the results; all present may then vote unanimously and so affirm group solidarity, amidst cries of *todo el pueblo*, or "the entire town."

3. *Self-disparagement.* This is a running down of oneself and anything with which he identifies. This can be done either by emphasizing the absence of positive values or the prevalence of negative ones. Disparagement is, "a denial of challenge, in the sense that the individual deprecates himself as unworthy of a serious effort or deprecates the values embodied in the challenge as undeserving of his best energies. He is not a failure because he did not try" (Cleaveland and Longaker 1957:195). This concept also has been applied in the study of psychiatric disorders in anomic communities as reported in "The Stirling County Study, Vol. II," where self-disparagement is described as, "a conviction of one's own incapacities and hence the hopelessness of all trying. Sentiments of this sort can be generated by being unloved and by the daily experience of being unable to exert control over events, of being always on the receiving end of action initiated by others rather than being an initiator" (Leighton 1960:416). In Ixtepeji, a common manner of talking about oneself is to dwell on poverty, ignorance, backwardness, weakness, and general crudeness. When identification is extended to the town level, the same qualities are stressed plus other undesirable social ills such as lack of charity, malicious gossip, and general lack of social grace. As suggested previously, this outward appearance must be examined in relation to the underlying motivation responsible for choosing to present such an image of self. One tenable reason is explained by Foster's related concepts of the "Principle of Equivalence" and the "Image of Limited Good" (Foster 1965a, 1965b). Assuming that Ixtepejanos, like the people of Tzintzuntzan described by Foster, are concerned lest their neighbors think they are rising above them in acquisition of desired goods, then it is logical for them to attempt to create the impression that such a thing is not occurring. Thus viewed, a deprecation of oneself is a strategy to combat the impression of others that he is rising above his proper position vis-a-vis these others. As such, self-disparagement may be a superficial, intentionally created mask that hides a different image of how any individual manifesting this behavior actually does perceive himself. At present, there is no way of resolving which of these two alternatives is the most correct with regard to Ixtepejanos.

In Ixtepeji this tendency to denigrate oneself is apparent in social interactions in which the object is to create the impression of being in a worse position or less worthwhile than the other person. (*cf.* Chapter 7). A visiting foreigner is an easy person with whom to play this game, since by local criteria he is obviously better off than anyone in the town; first of all, the visitor is not from such a "backward place"; he has enough wealth and power to be able to travel from "a very rich country," which is "more beautiful" than the local environment, which is "impoverished." It is also easy to make comparisons between the visitor's clothes and equipment and local types. Many such observations of material things are, of course, realistic, but comparisons are also made about the people themselves. A jest often made with a foreign visitor is that he should leave his "seed" in the town to reinforce the town blood, which is "very weak." This jest is in accord with the general idea that the "race" is getting weaker along with the general decrease in the fertility of the total environment.

Also, informants, when dismayed by the anthropologist's questions, attempt to excuse themselves by stressing their ignorance or stupidity and inability to understand such complicated things, since they have no way of knowing what "the truth" is. People who are unable to read are also likely to preface such remarks with, "To such a poor illiterate as I. . . ." An inevitable precursor to a meal in the house of new acquaintances is an apology by the host for the cuisine, which, as they often say, "We eat in our simplicity." Typical, too, is the custom of describing one's home as "my humble house," with the connotation of it being primitive and uncomfortable. "Humble" (*humilde*) is also frequently used in any speech referring to the town in general.

4. *Individualism.* A strong individualistic orientation in interpersonal relations achieves two ends: First, it minimizes potentially dangerous involvements; and second, it minimizes obligations to relatives and friends who would otherwise have claims on Ego. Banfield describes the same pattern in southern Italy.

> As the Montegranesi see it, friends and neighbors are not only potentially *costly* but potentially *dangerous* as well. No family, they think, can stand to see another prosper without feeling *envy*, and wishing the other harm. Friends and neighbors are, of course, peculiarly liable to envy, both because they know more about one's business than do others and because they feel themselves to be more directly in competition (1958:121; italics mine).

There are thus economic and psychological reasons for the individual to fall back on his own resources rather than participate in communal activities.

This individualism also affects family structure. The Ixtepeji family fits into the general picture of rural Mexican peasantry. It is bilateral and patripotestal with minimal extension of the kindred. The residence pattern following marriage is predominantly patrilocal. The newlyweds, however, invariably are anxious to have their own household and usually reside with the groom's parents for only one or two years, their departure often signaled by the birth of their first child. This particular type of individualism also exists within the nuclear family, affecting interpersonal relations, which are similar to Tepoztlán where, "Lack of trust is not only present among nonrelatives, but also exists within families and affects the relations of husbands and wives, parents and children, and brothers and sisters" (Lewis 1951:292).

The Ixtepejano thus limits the range of potentially functional kinship relations to the minimum necessary for procreation and unavoidable sex-based division of labor.[2] For example, this individualistic orientation affects inheritance patterns.

---

[2] Based in part on analysis of the "Relational Orientation," in a slightly altered Spanish Language version of the Value-Orientation Schedule (Kluckhohn and Strodtbeck 1961:368–378). N=25.

It is generally thought that the best arrangement brothers can make after the death of their father is for them to divide up his property in equal parts and manage them separately. The general explanation for this practice is that it is not possible for brothers, or any other two men, to manage their affairs together, that in such an arrangement one brother will inevitably get control over the share of the other(s), and therefore it is better that they maintain their interests apart. Ready access to communal lands in Ixtepeji has undoubtedly made such arrangements easier, thus inhibiting the development of strong extended families. As said above, fathers and grown sons can and often do live and work together, but such an arrangement only lasts while the son is willing to take orders from the father, since, "there can be only one head of the household." This situation is similar to nearby Juquila where, "kinsmen who work together continually must be related consanguineally (or adopted as consanguineal), and they must be lineally related" (Nader 1964:245). Talea seems to be another instance of this tendency to reduce kin-based associations, for there, "the family members who work together continually must be related both consanguineally and lineally, and the son must be unmarried" (*Ibid*:245).

Individualism, as a defensive strategy in a hostile world, can be stated as a proposition:

> Deemphasize all potential relationships except those absolutely necessary and thereby minimize the claims and threats of others.

The opposite logical alternative is not attempted:

> Intensify all potential relationships, so as to maximize security, and accept the resultant obligations and dangers incurred.

Is the first alternative adaptive? Chapter 13 takes up this question; let it suffice here to say that thematic content analysis of expressive activities displays a predominant concern with abandonment, betrayal, and death expressed from the solitary point of view of the lone individual. Indeed, solitude is preeminent, "the feeling and knowledge that one is alone, alienated from the world and oneself" (Paz 1959:175; my translation).

The above defensive strategies are four logically possible solutions to the problem of adjusting to the perceived hostile environment. That is, we can view them as answers to the problem of how to survive and make life bearable in the midst of deprivation made all the more apparent by the existence of a surrounding world thought to contain all that is desired. Thus, repression attempts to alleviate the problem by vanquishing awareness of it from consciousness. Conversely, the fiesta and similar activities are attempts to participate momentarily in an ideal environment. Thus, in differing contexts the individual identifies with either the positive or the negative. Both value systems are operative at all times, but it is a question of which predominates in consciousness. This ambivalence results from a logical inconsistency between two of the defensive strategies that in turn reduces their effectiveness, viz., disparagement is directly contrary to creating the ideal (although repression is necessary for creating the ideal).

These four defensive strategies are the ones that are apparent ethnographi-
cally; others may also be operative, but if so, have not been discerned. Logically,
however, other alternative compensations are possible. For example, one other
possibility is to attempt reducing the perceived negativity of the world by transforming it into the desired. The following chapter examines this and other possibilities.

Emotions and Philosophy of Life

So far we have mainly discussed the logical and outward aspects of how
Ixtepejanos come to terms with their environment. In earlier chapters we used
such terms as "fatalism," "resignation," and "present time orientation" to describe
how they are often immobilized in the face of uncomprehended and unpredictable forces that seem often to work against the lone individual. But we might also
ask (and this is the most difficult task in anthropology), what are the prevalent
emotions and internal experiences that color and give life and meaning to these
perceptions. In other words, what is the emotional and philosophical counterpart
of this view of life in which the world is seen as essentially empty of all that is
desirable?

A cross-culturally common response to deprivation in this world is an
optimistic attitude about death and the after life. Another response common in
societies suffering from severe social stress is the development of utopian faith
in the advent of a new age, or possibly the return of an earlier time when life was
better. But as we have seen from our examination of Ixtepeji religion and temporal
orientation, Ixtepejanos are hardheaded realists in these matters. Instead of seeing
death as a solution to problems on earth, they regard it as one more step in the
general dissolution of things. Suicide, as the reader will recall, is not therefore a
logical response to one's problems, and is virtually nonexistent in the Sierra Juárez.
Similarly there is little belief that the world of the living will improve.

In Chapter 10, which discussed drinking, we saw that one of the main motivations to drink was to heighten and intensify emotional experiences. We saw
also how the fiesta, as a cultural institution in Ixtepeji, provides a symbolic and
emotional milieu that also serves this same purpose. This proclivity to intensify
emotional experiences is consistent with other basic aspects of the world view
and may be seen as an adjustment to it and the underlying environmental conditions. Thus, if the future is seen as unpredictable and less desirable than the present,
and the past is seen as a more prosperous age that is irretrievably lost, then one is
left willy–nilly with the instantaneous present in which he must invest his existence
in order to validate life. Life, which at best is tenuous in Ixtepeji, is regarded in
the same manner as natural resources: one must exploit it now, in the present,
before the opportunity is lost. One does this by intensifying experience, by bom-
barding the senses, both inner and outer, with stimuli that intrude into consciousness and affirm one's existence. This same end seems to be furthered symbolically
by what seems to Anglo–Americans an obsession with death. By treating death
with frankness and by surrounding themselves with symbols of it Ixtepejanos affirm

the tenuousness of life, as though reminding themselves that time is short, that one must live now. This explains the supercharged emotionality of wakes, at which friends and relatives eat, drink, and sob at the feet of a cadaver stretched out in the midst of the feast, and also puts into perspective the emotional intensity surrounding the fiesta of Todos Santos.

This is not, however, something that is confined only to drinking and fiesta settings, but rather a dominant theme running through the entire culture, manifesting in an affinity for excitement, loud noises, bright colors, and emotionally stirring experiences, all of which are of course in the fiesta. One might even argue that the predilection for highly spiced food is consistent with this desire to stimulate the senses. We might also cite the high-pitched emotional content of radio dramas, popular music, and the bull fight, all of which figure so prominently in Mexican culture.

13

Prospects for Change

P RECEDING CHAPTERS show how in many areas of Ixtepeji life there are large discrepancies between "ideal" and "real" culture. This gap between desired conditions and those perceived as existing results in resignation and a lack of striving for goals which the world view defines as out of the reach of individuals. We can now further examine these beliefs and values plus some prospects for change in them.

Change in the Concept of Change

The existence of ideals is a statement about the future, for ideals are an optimistic faith in the ability of the present to transform to the desirable. By the same token, absence of meaningful ideals is consistent with fatalism and lack of optimism about the future. This is the situation in Ixtepeji where there is not only a strong sense of fatalism but the general belief that the future will bring conditions more undesirable than the present, the corollary of which is that change per se is undesirable since it is tending in this direction. Here there is an inversion of the predominant Anglo–American positive value on the future and the belief that change itself is desirable. Ixtepejanos believe that there are minor fluctuations in an overall tendency which will culminate eventually in the destruction of the entire world—the ultimate catastrophe. But these fluctuations are the result of capricious chance, or luck. This belief in chance is in accord with the capriciousness they attribute to the powers directing individual and group destiny. A more mechanical view of the world, such as that of the Navajo, precludes belief in luck; there, gambling and games of chance are not meaningful endeavors. But in contrast, consider the Mexican interest in gambling, especially the national lottery. If the world is largely understandable in terms of a machine, as for the Navajos, then knowledge of the rules that govern it is important. But for Ixtepejanos, knowledge in the fatalistic world of chance is of little value.

Looked at historically, these sentiments are not unrealistic, for conditions have often worsened. Also, immediate conditions tend to reinforce concern with the present. Surviving from day to day at a subsistence level requires intensive labor with little or no surplus energy, time, or resources with which to alter the future. This is also consistent with the value placed on the material versus the abstract, "something we can eat." It is not surprising therefore that prayers are by and large requests for material things and conditions in the present, not for ideals or virtues in the future. The belief that there is no life after death, except as a spirit wandering in an environment less desirable than earth, also reflects this present time orientation.

Extensive plans are not made for the future because there are problems enough in the present, and then of what avail are plans if the future is essentially indeterminate? There are, for example, no fortune telling techniques, except ones that forebode bleak futures. Speaking subjectively, there seems to be a strong desire to somehow immobilize the present, to affirm the moment that forever has the potential to transpire into sudden disaster, "a great indescribable *susto*," as one informant said. The spontaneous shout, the burst of rockets, the shooting off of pistols, the yelping cry of a kicked dog, all serve to shatter the lugubrious atmosphere of *la soledad*, and they do this by occurring in the instantaneous present. As a local proverb says, "We are here today, but who knows about tomorrow."

Another main orientation is the particular type of individualism whereby the individual tends to rely primarily on his own resources rather than joining forces with others.[1] This results in the absence of viable corporate structures, the only exceptions being those resulting when the town is forced to close ranks for mutual protection in the face of perceived external threats, rather than for generalized benefit. Aside from the explanation that involvement with others is perceived as dangerous because of the potential lowering of defenses that it requires, we might go so far as to argue that the notion of a group is in a sense an abstraction and as such less "real" than the directly experienced self, which, in a world of *engaño* and *ilusión*, is the only thing that can be trusted. Furthermore, reinforcing this tendency toward individualism, (the tendency not to enter into corporate association), is the underlying assumption that such associations are ineffectual in the face of overwhelming forces, which can cancel out the best laid plans of men at whim.

One way of looking at the impediments to desirable change in Ixtepeji is to consider how it is out of alignment with the mentalities of the urban, industrial world that it views with so much ambivalence. As we have seen, some of these differences prevent Ixtepejanos from coming together to solve basic material problems that are a prerequisite for a better life, which all agree is painfully lacking.

---

[1] The most common exceptions to this are short-term contractual arrangements, rarely among more than two persons. A more enduring dyadic relation is formalized in a *guelagueza* relationship, whereby two individuals, or households, agree to reciprocally loan various goods and services, interest free. Accounts of the transactions are recorded in ledgers, and repayment may be requested at any time. Absent is the Zapotec mutual aid arrangement of *gozona* (*cf.* De La Fuente 1949:146–147, and Nader 1964:247–249).

To begin with, there must be a readjustment in the very way in which they think of change. That is, the potential for improvement must somehow be demonstrated. Presumably with greater contact and involvement with the outside world, their time orientations will give way to a more typically modern, linear concept. The dominant time orientation emphasizes the present and past versus the future and sees yearly time as basically a cyclical repetition of events in the agricultural and ritual calendar. Somehow individuals must also realize the desirability and feasibility of coming together for corporate action to promote desired change. The strong individualism need not necessarily be an impediment to this, for individualism has not prevented the development of cooperative group formation elsewhere. But there must be a readjustment of the perception of the individual in relation to others. In both the modern Western and the Ixtepeji brand of individualism, there is the same structural feature of the self perceiving itself as split off from the rest of the world, but the two types are mirror images of each other. In both, the self–world dichotomy exists, but whereas the man of the modern Western world perceives himself as dominant over nature and much of the world, the Ixtepeji situation is reversed such that the self is submissive.[2]

Most thinking about economic and social development is implicitly based on the Western concept of progress. Central to this thinking and set of values is the belief in the desirability of man establishing dominance over a subdued natural world. The long range adaptability of this attitude and stance toward nature is currently being questioned as evidence accumulates that the technological giants of the modern world have created nonviable modes of relating to the natural environment. The life diminishing effects of pollution and overcrowding that are now blighting urban centers of the modern world are still relatively slight in Ixtepeji, and the case could be made that the Ixtepejanos's poverty and ineffectiveness to alter the natural landscape at will are potentially a more adaptive way of life than the voracious consumerism of the middle and upper classes. This is not to argue against introducing technological change into Ixtepeji and other similarly damaged ecosystems, but rather to do so in ways that do not merely replicate the practices and values of the modern Western world. It is ironic that modern technology is the cause of many of the current ecological catastrophes, of which Ixtepeji is only one of thousands of examples, and at the same time offers the only foreseeable way out. Modern technology itself is neither malignant nor benign, only uses of it are, as the great industrial powers are now beginning to discover. Hopefully, the so-called "newly developing" areas of the world, such as Ixtepeji, are in a position to benefit from the "mistakes of progress" of these more affluent countries, and in doing so can establish more harmonious and adaptive relationships with their natural environments.

What follows are a few suggestions that seem, at least to me after some years of acquaintances with Ixtepeji, to be both feasible and ecologically sound in the long run.

---

[2] Based in part on analysis of the "Man–Nature Orientation," in a slightly altered Spanish Language version of the Value-Orientation Schedule (Kluckhohn and Strodtbeck 1961:368–378). N=25.

A Strategy for Development

In forming a strategy for change the first assumption must be that outside assistance will be minimal. The inability of government agencies to invest in the local setting is a situation that cannot be expected to change in the near future.[3] The current income received from the paper company logging in the mountains of the municipio is a temporary activity that does not enter into any long-range picture aside from the possibility that, as a result of overcutting, it may eventually

[3] For a discussion of the most extensive program of economic and social assistance in the region, *cf.* Poleman (1964).

Tequio repairing bridge damaged by high waters.

harm the environment. Although unlikely, it is conceivable that someday outside interests might reopen the mines of the municipio. This would provide employment, but since the municipio does not hold the mineral rights, most of the profits would leave the town. Other communities both in the Sierra and the Valley of Oaxaca have partially adjusted to land pressure and flagging economies by building up indigenous craft industries. Folk crafts and artisans that produce them are, however, absent in Ixtepeji, and as such are not a significant potential economic base.

These conditions point to the conclusion that solutions to improve the currently backsliding economy must be built on existing economic and human resources. This means that the people of Ixtepeji must expect to depend primarily on farming for some time to come; the crucial issue here is of course corn. If corn, as we saw in Chapter 1, is maladapted to the local environment, it is at least better suited than any other crop that the people are now economically prepared to accept. At present a man with access to several hectares for corn cultivation is reasonably well assured of at least a subsistence existence, but it is almost impossible to rise above this level without some form of assistance. The way out of this dependency on corn must ultimately be through crop diversification which includes cash crops as well as subsistence ones. Some years ago the Papaloapan Commisssion introduced some fruit trees, mainly peach and quince, in the *agencia* of San Pedro Nexicho, where they are now grown on a limited basis. These small orchards plus larger experimental ones developed in Ixtlán by a North American resident, who is a botanist, have demonstrated to the people of Ixtepeji the suitability of orchard industries for their needs. Both in terms of soil erosion and soil exhaustion, fruit trees are profoundly less detrimental than corn to the fragile soils on the steep slopes of the area. The immediate obstacle is, however, capitalization. Even assuming that one has the money necessary to start an orchard, he is faced with the prospect of having the land used not producing for four to five years until the trees began to bear fruit. This is an investment that no one in the town is currently in a position to make, except on a small scale that provides for little more than household consumption.

As for credit arrangements, at present almost all credit is provided for short terms at high rates by money lenders in the town. Bank credit is virtually nonexistent for agricultural purposes. While the government-operated Banco Nacional de Crédito Ejidal controls the funds received by the municipio from the paper company and matches them for public works (such as the water system and school), it has not been active in extending credit to individuals in the area. Nor have the limited credit programs of the Papaloapan Commission, which have been active mainly in the Gulf Coast area, been extended to Ixtepeji and many other communities on the periphery of the Papaloapan Basin (*cf.* Poleman 1964). Clearly, this lack of credit facilities is also one of the main obstacles to agricultural development in Ixtepeji.

The desirability of diversifying into fruit trees again brings the subsistence cultivation of corn back into focus. Since the leap from corn to fruit trees or other crops is at present too large to make, the people must find ways of improving the corn base of the economy such that it will support other developments. In earlier pages we have discussed the "fatalism" with which Ixtepejanos view so much of their lives, but here it must be noted that such an attitude does not seem to be greatly involved in a slowness to employ more productive techniques. Ixtepejanos are reasonably aware of various technical means to improve production; the limiting factors as they see them are, first of all, lack of economic resources necessary to buy and maintain farm machinery, which in any event would be useless on the steep slopes where they are forced to plant. Furthermore, aside from lack of money to buy machinery and expensive fertilizers, they are often discouraged by the technical knowledge which, lacking special education, they feel incapable of acquiring.

The present relatively ineffective and even destructive methods of corn cultivation in the Sierra Juárez can in part be explained historically. As we discussed earlier, corn cultivation was for centuries practiced as an adaptation of a low density population to large expanses of land that permitted an extensive agriculture. In the absence of severe land pressure, which is a recent development, more intensive techniques, such as are common for example in areas of the Old World which have been densely populated for thousands of years, were not developed. Thus, such agricultural practices as crop rotation, household truck gardening, an efficient use of animal, human, and wood ash fertilizer, and composting are conspicuously absent in Ixtepeji. As for a suitable crop to rotate with corn, alfalfa is grown in the municipio, mainly on solares in the town where with irrigation it yields a year round supplement to feed domestic animals. As of yet, however, no one has experimented with sowing fallow milpas with it as a means of erosion control and soil enrichment.

Since the above mentioned intensive agricultural techniques are absent primarily due to historic and cultural reasons rather than economic ones, there

Deforestration and erosion on hillside above town.

is good reason to believe that with proper demonstration of their effectiveness, Ixtepejanos will readily accept them. The following incident illustrates both the readiness and willingness of men in the town to experiment with new techniques given the opportunity and an acceptable level of risk. In April 1970 I discussed at length with several men in the town experimental milpas planted by the botanist in Ixtlán, using essentially local techniques and strains of corn. By the judicious use of artificial and natural fertilizers he was able to double and even triple his yield above normal. Two of these men from Ixtepeji later returned with me to the experimental milpas in Ixtlán where the owner spent one half of a day instructing us in the use of fertilizers and how to set out small experimental plots. The three of us then returned to Ixtepeji with samples of fertilizer and great enthusiasm to begin the experiments. Apparently due to the variety of soils used for planting, the results were quite variable; they were, however, good enough to encourage the two Ixtepejanos to continue experimenting.

While there is a readiness to accept small scale, low risk technical innovations, one can expect to find much greater resistance to rearranging existing social relations along potentially sounder economic lines. Earlier we had occasion to discuss the strong individualism of Ixtepejanos and their great value on personally controlling their private affairs. This, probably more than any one other thing, inhibits the formation of cooperatives and other mutual aid organizations. It is interesting to speculate, for example, on what increase in the total agricultural output of the community could be gained merely by combining some of the hundreds of small privately tilled fields that checkerboard the landscape, thus making available many areas of land currently devoted to fencing and paths, and also allowing for more efficient plowing and planting.

Corn fodder stored in trees.

The Beginning of Innovation
and Cooperation

The fertilizer experiment mentioned above demonstrates that the idea of improving local conditions is not completely absent, for the possibility is held to exist. It is rather that most of the people realize they do not have the economic resources that they consider necessary, nor the knowledge and abilities to acquire such wealth. At present they look mainly to the old mines, new industry, and irrigation projects as the main possibilities for change, but they hold out little hope that such things will happen in the foreseeable future. But, at the same time, they are frustrated by the belief that government agencies have the power to perform such acts at will, should they be so inclined. Here is the same theme, common also in the content of dreams and folktales, that some very desirable thing is just out of reach—so near and yet so far.

One factor in the "opening up" of some individuals is the relative degree of social and political stability of the last generation. This has made possible the beginning of the development of a sense of security within the village. But, at the same time, external conditions have been working against this. Most important here is the realization of the townspeople that they are being left behind in the general progress that this stability has afforded the "more comfortable classes." Political rhetoric, which speaks of the progress of the "humble classes," further aggravates this sense of relative deprivation and nourishes a cynicism toward planned change.

Any alterations in basic orientations discussed above will have to come about first in individuals, people who are innovators. Most existing values are not conducive to innovation. Fear of newness, of the strange, and a desire to cling to the minimal security of the past and present create an atmosphere in which innovation does not flourish. On the contrary, if it does appear, it is apt to be stifled, as in the case of Beatriz Delgado. Beatriz is a young woman who by personal initiative and family aid obtained teaching credentials and returned to town to teach. But tastes and styles she acquired in the city created such a stir of condemnation that life in Ixtepeji was unbearable for her. She is a good illustration of Mering's statement that, "It is the innovator in any given culture who most often finds himself in this field of ambiguity and experiences it most acutely" (1961:84). Beatriz's solution to these pressures, as in the case of many others who find themselves out of tune with local patterns, was to leave town. The widening cultural gulf between these urbanized Ixtepejanos and their mountain relatives is painfully evident to all whenever the emigrants return home for visits, such as during a recent town fiesta when approximately 100 of them traveled and arrived together. They were well received but not without suspicion and uneasiness.

For those who remain in the town and those that leave to seek their fortunes elsewhere, there is the same ambivalence about the outside world. It is a dilemma between a desire for escape from the monotony and drudgery of village life and a fear of losing the minimal security, which it provides. Individuals must choose between continuing to eke out a day-to-day existence in the local environment, perceived as essentially devoid of potential for improvement, and taking the risk of seeking their fortune in the outside world, which is the repository of much of what they desire. This dilemma is greatest for young adults who have had early awareness of the discrepancy between the quality of village life and what is possible outside. Unmarried young people unanimously desire to leave the town, "to get a good job and make money." This desire of the town's best youth to leave is perhaps the biggest problem, for few who leave ever return.

A recent development seems to be, in part, a reversal of the strong individual orientation impeding cooperative action. This was a change in the method for sponsoring the annual town fiesta in honor of the patron saint. Until ten years ago, the fiesta expenses were funded by a system known as the *padrinaje*, whereby forty or fifty "godfathers of the fiesta" each donated about 50 pesos. Under the new method of financing, every adult male contributes a minimum of 15 pesos. Since there were 300 contributors in 1966, the figure came to 4500 pesos, which is considerably more than was usual under the old system. Everyone is quick to point out that although in some respects the fiesta has deteriorated, for example the fiesta procession is not as long and the traditional dances not as good, it is nevertheless more "luxurious" because of the extra money, which goes for more fireworks, mezcal, and tepache. The expenses for the 1966 fiesta rose to over 6000 pesos, necessitating an additional assessment to cover the deficit not taken care of by contributions from the Mexico City visitors.

This change in fiesta sponsorship points up two conflicting tendencies. On one hand, it is part of the slow but progressive breakdown in the traditional *mayordomía* system for fiesta sponsorship, which anthropologists have depicted as a "leveling mechanism" impeding the accumulation of capital goods in the hands of would-be innovators and entrepreneurs. A similar shift from *mayordomo* to *barrio* sponsorship has occurred in several towns of the nearby *rincón* area as well (*cf.* Nader 1964:237). But in Ixtepeji, although there is this tendency for release of individuals from the burden of the fiesta sponsorship, considered on the level of the entire town, the new system is even more retrogressive in terms of dissipation of capital. Whereas the mayordomía system dissipated the resources of individuals, the new system disposes of a considerably greater sum of the town's total capital resources. This decision to so channel scarce resources into the annual fiesta is an implicit value statement of priorities for resource expenditure. It reflects the prevalent belief that it is futile to attempt to improve local conditions economically, that a better way to make life more livable is by having better fiestas.

Although the picture of Ixtepeji's future is bleak, it is not without hope, for there are occasional individuals who are willing to risk experimenting with new agricultural practices. In 1966 two men, who are progressive by local standards, planted the first hybrid corn in the town's history. They conceived the idea themselves after seeing demonstration plots in Guelatao. It is significant that one of them, a school teacher, has spent considerable time in Oaxaca City, where he was educated. The experiment was a failure due to lack of rain and the corn variety being unsuitable for the local conditions. Both men suffered heavy financial losses because of the failure, but nevertheless are still interested in making more agricultural experiments.

A crucial factor in this corn venture is that it was a cooperative endeavor, although a minimal one. Because the men pooled their financial resources and labor, they were able to undertake the experiment which, in face of the uncertainties involved, most individuals would not attempt alone.

Several other recent cooperative ventures illustrate both some of the problems involved and also some of the necessary ingredients for success. In early 1968 a man in the town was able to acquire a truck on credit, which he used for hauling passengers and cargo to and from Oaxaca. In this way he was able to make his payments and clear a small profit. After a short time he sold it to buy a larger truck, which he used mainly for hauling men to logging camps in the mountains and also for hauling wood for the paper company. Upon seeing his success four other men decided to form an association to buy another truck, which they did, using it for the same purpose. But after several months a violent conflict developed among them in which municipal authorities had to intervene, with the result that one of the men was forced out of the association. Meanwhile the trucking business of the first man was prospering, such that he became the subject of much envy and rumors that he had killed a young man of the town who had recently died a mysterious death. Although life was made difficult for him, the successes of his enterprise apparently made it worthwhile to the point where he invested in another truck. Meanwhile, the man who was forced out of the association came back into the competition for local business by putting a down payment on a truck of his own, apparently using profits he had made from his brief association in the four-man venture. By now there were four trucks in the town and people were rapidly becoming accustomed to their service, such that a movement was started to have the town itself buy one. This was finally achieved, and the new truck was duly christened with the name of Coquelay, in honor of the sixteenth century *cacique* of the town, with the name being painted in large letters on the hood. By now many more people were beginning to see advantages of the trucks. Potential business thus appeared great enough that the three associates invested in a second one, bringing the total for the town up to six. Thus, in less than two years the coming and going of the trucks in the town has become a regular event, and in a year or so people will probably no longer stop work to look up and note them as they come backfiring down the mountain side. Already they have had a perceptible effect on the town. Men who do much trading and hauling further back in the mountains now find it easier to get their cargoes into Oaxaca City by putting them on the truck of a fellow townsman at a roadhead, thus eliminating two or three days of leading their animals on the trails. Eventually the trucks will reduce the horse, mule, and burro population in the municipio, and thus give some relief to the land. People in the town are also beginning to see a profit in making rapid trips to the market in Oaxaca with small quantities of low margin produce such as flowers, surplus corn, fruit, chickens, eggs, and so forth. Buses passing the highway above the town provide transportation to Oaxaca City, but to use them there is the problem of getting the merchandise up the four-and-one-half kilometer road to the bus stop, since the buses are unable to enter the town as the trucks do. Also the bus rates are considerably higher for both passengers and cargo, and in the case of cargo there is a limit on quantity that can be boarded. The trucks will thus presumably stimulate increased production of cash crops, especially perishable fruits, which will find a market in the increasing growth of Oaxaca City.

The next decade will most likely reveal whether Ixtepeji will be able to survive as a viable farming community. If it is to do so, current trends of soil erosion and population pressure on the land must be altered through adjustments in agriculture, life style, and outlook. The bleak alternative would seem to be increased economic decline and emigration from the *municipio* into the slums of Oaxaca City, Mexico City, and other swelling urban areas.

14

Summary

THIS STUDY has followed two approaches in examining Ixtepeji society, its ideas, and values. The primary one has shown how various traits are founded on beliefs and values that depict an existence that is far from what is desired, and also that this situation is most realistically thought of in terms of cultural pathology. Here we as scientists are entering the realm of values ourselves, but at least we are not at odds with the people on this point. We also saw how the internal logic of the community is self-perpetuating. The main argument here was that various defensive strategies such as deception, individualism, and drinking, along with other institutionalized modes of behavior such as envy, distrust, skepticism, fatalism, and witchcraft tend to perpetuate the very qualities of interpersonal relations that are held to be undesirable and perception of which is also projected onto the nonhuman environment. In short, the social milieu can be seen in terms of a complex feedback system in which individuals who are attempting to protect themselves from threats and dangers they perceive, usually realistically, in the social and geographical environment, take defensive measures that create, within the context of the total society, the very conditions they seek to escape.

Whereas the preceding analysis is static and assumes a closed system, we also examined historical and external conditions that introduce genetic factors. Here to a great extent Ixtepeji is a microcosm of Mexico in general, which Tannenbaum characterizes as "peculiarly tragic, violent, and remorseless. At various times the Mexican people have seen the sudden apparition of an enigmatic evil that destroyed whatever made life worth living" (1962:17).

It could have been possible in this study to have given more attention to more amicable sides of Ixtepeji culture. But, the emphasis on negative aspects of life in the Sierra Juárez has been in the attempt to get at the most salient features. In this regard, this interpretation is in agreement with the people of Ixtepeji. This is how they tell it.

Glossary

Agencia: A territorial and administrative subunit of a *municipio.*
Ayuntamiento: The municipal government; also refers to the municipal government building.
Barrio: A district or ward of a town. In Ixtepeji *barrio* members do not necessarily live in the *barrio* to which they belong.
Bracero: A farm worker, especially one who has worked in the United States.
Cabecera: The seat of a *distrito.*
Cacique: A rural political boss, especially one of Indian descent.
Cargo: An official position in either the civil or religious hierarchies of the *municipio* and its *agencias.*
Compadrazgo: Ritual co-parenthood between the parents of a child and the godparents of the child.
Curandero: A folk healer.
Desconfianza: Distrust; suspicion.
Distrito: A territorial and administrative unit comparable to a county.
Elote: An ear of soft corn.
Encomendero: The holder of the title to an *encomienda.* The encomienda was an early colonial institution in which use rights to lands and the labor of people living on them were granted by the Spanish Crown to favored subjects.
Engaño: Deception; trickery; treachery; lure.
Fanega: A variable Spanish unit of land surface area.
Hectare: A unit of land surface area equal to 2.47 acres.
Ilusión: An illusion; a disheartening experience.
Macho: A man who possesses *machismo.*
Machismo: Refers to strongly masculine characteristics, especially courage, pride, and sexual prowess.
Maíz: Corn (*Zea mays*).
Mayordomo: A sponsor of a fiesta or some other ceremonial event; this system of sponsorship is called *mayordomía.*
Mazorca: An ear of corn.
Metate: A grinding or milling stone.
Mezcal: An alcoholic beverage distilled from the maguey plant (*Agave spp.*).
Milpa: A corn field.
Monte: As used in Ixtepeji it usually refers to forest areas of the higher elevations.

135

Municipio: A territorial and administrative unit intermediate between an *agencia* and a *distrito.*

Olla: A ceramic cooking pot.

Petate: A woven reed sleeping mat.

Rincón: Refers to a Zapotec area in the mountains east of Ixtepeji.

Serrano: Refers to persons or dialects of the mountains.

Solar: An irrigated plot of land in or near the center of the town.

Soledad: Solitude; loneliness.

Susto: A sudden fright which may cause loss of the soul or other illness.

Tepache: A fermented drink made from juice of the maguey plant (*Agave spp.*).

Tequio: A communal work party.

Tiendita: Dimunitive of *tienda,* a store.

References

ADAMS, RICHARD N., and ARTHUR J. RUBEL, 1967, "Sickness and Social Relations."
In *Handbook of Middle American Indians*. Robert Wauchope (ed.). Austin, Tex.:
University of Texas Press. 6:333–356.

ALBERT, ETHEL, 1956, "The Classification of Values: A Method and Illustration."
American Anthropologist 58:221–248.

BANFIELD, EDWARD C., 1958, *The Moral Basis of a Backward Society*. Glencoe, Ill.:
The Free Press.

BENEDICT, RUTH, 1959 (1934), *Patterns of Culture*. New York: New American
Library.

BOHANNAN, PAUL, 1963, *Social Anthropology*. New York: Holt, Rinehart and
Winston.

BUNZEL, R., 1940, "The Role of Alcoholism in Two Central American Cultures."
Psychiatry 3:361–387.

CANCIAN, FRANK, 1965, *Economics and Prestige in a Maya Community*. Stanford,
Calif.: Stanford University Press.

CLEAVELAND, E. J. and W. D. LONGAKER, 1957, "Neurotic Patterns in the Family." In
Explorations in Social Psychiatry. Alexander Leighton (ed.). New York: Basic
Books, 167–200.

COHEN, YEHUDI A., 1961, "Food and Its Vissitudes: A Cross-Cultural Study of Sharing and Nonsharing." In *Social Structure and Personality*, by Yehudi A. Cohen.
New York: Holt, Rinehart and Winston, 312–350.

CUADROS SINÓPTICOS, COLECCIÓN DE, 1883, *De los Pueblos, Haciendas, y Ranchos
del Estado Libre y Soberano de Oaxaca*. Oaxaca: Imprenta del Estado.

CURRIER, RICHARD L., 1966, "The Hot–Cold Syndrome and Symbolic Balance in
Mexican and Spanish–American Folk Medicine." Ethnology 5:251–263.

DE LA FUENTE, JULIO, 1949, *Yalalag: Una Villa Zapoteca Serrana*. Mexico: Museo
Nacional de Antropología.

FIELD, P. B., 1962, "A New Cross-Cultural Study of Drunkenness." In *Society, Culture,
and Drinking Patterns*. D. Pittman and C. P. Snyder (eds.). New York: Wiley,
48–74.

FISCHER, J. L., 1963, "The Sociopsychological Analysis of Folktales." *Current Anthropology* 4:235–273.

FOSTER, GEORGE M., 1944, "Nagualism in Mexico and Guatemala." *Acta Americana*
2:85–103.

137

————, 1953, "Relationships between Spanish and Spanish–American Folk Medicine." *Journal of American Folklore* 66:201–217.

————, 1965a, "Cultural Responses to Expressions of Envy in Tzintzuntzan." *Southwestern Journal of Anthropology* 21:24–35.

————, 1965b, "Peasant Society and the Image of Limited Good." *American Anthropologist* 67:293–315.

GAY, JOSE ANTONIO, 1950, *Historia de Oaxaca.* Mexico: Talleres V. Venero.

GILLIN, JOHN, 1948, "Magical Fright." *Psychiatry* 11:387–400.

HAMMEL, EUGENE A., 1967, "The Jewish Mother in Serbia or Les Structures Alimentaires de la Parenté." In *Essays in Balkan Ethnology.* Kroeber Anthropological Society Special Publication, No. 1, 55–62.

HEATH, D. B., 1958, "Drinking Patterns of the Bolivian Camba." *Quarterly Journal of Studies on Alcohol* 19:491–508.

HENDRY, JEAN CLARE, 1957, "Atzompa: A Pottery Producing Village of Southern Mexico," Ph.D. Dissertation. Ann Arbor, Mich.: University Microfilms.

HOLLAND, WILLIAM R., 1961, "El Tonalismo y El Nagualismo entre los Tzotziles de Larráinzar, Chiapas, Mexico." *Estudios de Cultura Maya* 1:167–181.

HOLMBERG, ALLAN R., 1960, *Nomads of the Long Bow: The Siriono of Eastern Bolivia.* Institute of Social Anthropology, Publication No. 10. Washington, D.C.: Smithsonian Institution.

HORCASITAS, FERNANDO and D. BUTTERWORTH, 1963, "La Llorona." *Tlalocan: Revista de Fuentes para el Conocimiento de las Culturas Indígenas de México* 4:204–224.

HORTON, DONALD, 1943, "The Functions of Alcohol in Primitive Societies: A Cross-Cultural Study." *Quarterly Journal of Studies on Alcohol* 4:199–320.

ITURRIBARRÍA, JORGE FERNANDO, 1955, *Oaxaca en la Historia.* Mexico: Editorial Stylo.

KEARNEY, MICHAEL, 1969, "An Exception to the 'Image of Limited Good.'" *American Anthropologist* 71:888–890.

KLUCKHOHN, CLYDE, 1951, "Values and Value-Orientation in the Theory of Action." In *Toward a General Theory of Action.* Parsons and Shils (eds.). New York: Harper & Row, 388–433.

KLUCKHOHN, FLORENCE R. and FRED L. STRODTBECK, 1961, *Variations in Value-Orientations.* New York: Harper & Row.

LEACH, E. R., 1954, *Political Systems of Highland Burma.* Boston: Beacon.

LEIGHTON, ALEXANDER H., 1960, *People of Cove and Woodlot.* The Stirling County Study of Psychiatric Disorder and Sociocultural Environment, Vol. II. New York: Basic Books.

LESLIE, CHARLES, 1960, *Now We Are Civilized: A Study of the World View of the Zapotec Indians of Mitla, Oaxaca.* Detroit: Wayne State University Press.

LEWIS, OSCAR, 1951, *Life in a Mexican Village: Tepoztlán Restudied.* Urbana, Ill.: University of Illinois Press.

MADSEN, WILLIAM, 1964, *Mexican–Americans of South Texas.* New York: Holt, Rinehart and Winston.

MADSEN, WILLIAM and C. MADSEN, 1969, "The Cultural Structure of Mexican Drinking Behavior." *Quarterly Journal of Studies on Alcohol* 30:701–718.

MANGIN, WILLIAM, 1957, "Drinking among Andean Indians." *Quarterly Journal of Studies on Alcohol* 18:55–65.

MAQUET, JACQUES J., 1964, "Some Epistemological Remarks on the Cultural Philosophies and their Comparison." In *Cross-Cultural Understanding: Epistemology in Anthropology.* F. S. C. Northrop, (ed.). New York: Harper & Row, 13–31.

MAUSS, MARCEL, 1967 (1925), *The Gift Forms and Functions of Exchange in Archaic Societies,* Ian Cunnison, (transl.). New York: Norton.

MERING, OTTO VON, 1961, *A Grammar of Human Values.* Pittsburgh, Pa.: University of Pittsburgh Press.

NADER, LAURA, 1964, *Talea and Juquila: A Comparison of Zapotec Social Organization.* Berkeley, Calif.: University of California Publications in American Archaeology and Ethnology, Vol. 48.

NIETZSCHE, FRIEDRICH, 1872, *Die Geburt der Tragödie aus dem Geiste der Musik.*

O'NELL, CARL W. and HENRY A. SELBY, 1968, "Sex Differences in the Incidence of Susto in Two Zapotec Pueblos: An Analysis of the Relationships between Sex Role Expectations and a Folk Illness." *Ethnology* 7:95–105.

PARSONS, ELSIE CLEWS, 1936, *Mitla, Town of Souls.* Chicago: University of Chicago Press.

PAZ, OCTAVIO, 1959, *El Laberinto de la Soledad.* Mexico: Fondo de Cultura.

PÉREZ GARCÍA, ROSENDO, 1956, *La Sierra Juárez.* Mexico: Grafica Cervantia.

PLATT, B. S., 1955, "Some Traditional Alcoholic Beverages and their Importance in the Indigenous African Communities." *Proceedings of the Nutrition Society* 14:115–124.

POLEMAN, THOMAS T., 1964, *The Papaloapan Project, Agricultural Development in the Mexican Tropics.* Stanford, Calif.: Stanford University Press.

RICHARDS, AUDREY L., 1964 (1932), *Hunger and Work in a Savage Tribe: A Functional Study of Nutrition among the Southern Bantu.* New York: Meridian.

ROMNEY, KIMBALL and ROMAINE ROMNEY, 1966, *The Mixtecans of Juxtlahuaca, Mexico.* New York: Wiley.

RUBEL, ARTHUR J., 1964, "The Epidemiology of a Folk Illness: *Susto* in Hispanic America." *Ethnology* 3:268–283.

————, 1966, *Across the Tracks Mexican–Americans in a Texas City.* Austin, Tex.: University of Texas Press.

SADLER, WILLIAM S., 1953, *Practice of Psychiatry.* St. Louis, Mo.: Mosby.

SIMMONS, OZZIE G., 1960, "Ambivalence and the Learning of Drinking Behavior in a Peruvian Community." *American Anthropologist* 62:1018–1027.

TAMAYO, CARLOS, 1956, *Oaxaca en la Revolución.* Mexico.

TANNENBAUM, FRANK, 1950, *Mexico: The Struggle for Peace and Bread.* New York: Knopf.

VILLA ROJAS, ALFONSO, 1963, "El Nagualismo como Recurso de Control Social entre los Grupos Mayances de Chiapas, México." *Estudios de Cultura Maya* 3:243–260.

VOGT, EVON Z., 1965, "Zinacanteco 'Souls.'" *Man* 65:33–35.

WHITING, JOHN W. M. and IRWIN L. CHILD, 1953, *Child Training and Personality: A Cross-Cultural Study.* New Haven, Conn.: Yale University Press.

WISDOM, CHARLES, 1940, *The Chorti Indians of Guatemala.* Chicago: University of Chicago Press.

Recommended Reading

DE LA FUENTE, JULIO, 1949, *Yalalag: Una Villa Zapoteca Serrana*. Mexico: Museo Nacional de Antropología. An ethnography of another Sierra Zapotec town which is more traditionally Zapotec than Ixtepeji.

FOSTER, GEORGE M., 1967, *Tzintzuntzan: Mexican Peasants in a Changing World*. Boston: Little, Brown. A many faceted book, both ethnographic and theoretical, based on long experience in a Tarascan Indian town in the state of Michoacán.

LEWIS, OSCAR, 1963, *Life in a Mexican Village: Tepoztlán Restudied*. Urbana: University of Illinois Press (originally published in 1951). An in-depth description of a Mexican peasant town in the state of Morelos. Also see Lewis' later book in which he pays particular attention to culture changes occurring there: *Tepoztlán: Village in Mexico*. New York: Holt, Rinehart and Winston, 1960.

NADER, LAURA, 1964, *Talea and Juquila: A Comparison of Zapotec Social Organization*. Berkeley, Calif.: University of California Publications, in *American Archaeology and Ethnology* Vol. 48, Number 3. This description of these nearby towns throws light on the social organization of Ixtepeji.

————, 1969, "The Zapotec of Oaxaca." In *Handbook of Middle American Indians*, Vol. 7, pp. 329–359. Robert Wauchope, General Editor. Austin, Tex. University of Texas Press. A synopsis of traditional Zapotec society and culture with good bibliographic references.

PARSONS, ELSIE CLEWS, 1936, *Mitla: Town of Souls and Other Zapotec-Speaking Pueblos of Oaxaca Mexico*. Chicago: University of Chicago Press. A detailed ethnography of a major town in the Valley of Oaxaca.

WOLF, ERIC R., 1959, *Sons of the Shaking Earth*. Chicago: University of Chicago Press. A good introduction to the historic and ethnographic complexity of Mexico.